The Irrepressible Automobile

The Irrepressible

A Freewheeling Jaunt Through the

Automobile

Fascinating World of the Motorcar

Vernon Pizer

Dodd, Mead & Company New York

For Adair

And the song, from beginning to end,
I found again in the heart of a friend.
—Henry Wadsworth Longfellow

Distributed in Canada by McClelland and Stewart Limited, Toronto
Manufactured in the United States of America

1 2 3 4 5 6 7 8 9 10

Library of Congress Cataloging-in-Publication Data

Pizer, Vernon, date
The irrepressible automobile.

Includes index.
Summary: A history of the automobile discussing some of the fallout it has spawned, such as parking problems and vanity tags, and emphasizing man's love affair with this motorized vehicle from the beginning.
1. Automobiles—Juvenile literature. [1. Automobiles] I. Title.
TL147.P59 1986 629.2'222 85-25239
ISBN 0-396-08580-6

There are many who have had a hand in the making of this book—some of them by intent, but some of them unwittingly. Some date back to the distant past, like Arnold Gingrich, founding editor of *Esquire*, who taught me that an ancient and decrepit Volkswagen can be a thing of joy, Harmon Boyette who put me into the driver's seat of the first luxury car to be imported into post-World War II Europe, and Johann Nekut who demonstrated to me just how much man can love his wheels. Some of them are of more recent vintage, like Derwood A. Haines of the Ford Motor Company, Richard Harper of the Chrysler Corporation, and Plina M. Doyle of the National Highway Traffic Safety Administration. I am grateful to all of them. If any flaws have crept into the text the sin is mine, not theirs.

VERNON PIZER
Valdosta, Georgia

Other Books by Vernon Pizer

EAT THE GRAPES DOWNWARD
An Uninhibited Romp Through the Surprising World of Food

TAKE MY WORD FOR IT

GLORIOUS TRIUMPHS
Athletes Who Conquered Adversity

SHORTCHANGED BY HISTORY:
America's Neglected Innovators

YOU DON'T SAY:
How People Communicate Without Speech

INK, ARK., AND ALL THAT:
How American Places Got Their Names

THE UNITED STATES ARMY

THE WORLD OCEAN:
Man's Last Frontier

THE USEFUL ATOM
(with William R. Anderson)

ROCKETS, MISSILES AND SPACE

Contents

1
It All Began in Susa

Go near, and join thyself to this chariot.
—Acts 8:29

If one insists on being hairsplittingly precise about how the whole thing got started, it is well to go back more than 5,000 years to the city of Susa near the mouth of the Tigris River in a region known to the ancient Jews as Elam. Archaeological findings at the site reveal the earliest known existence of the wheel. And if it were not for the wheel, humanity would find itself perched on a saddle instead of a bucket seat because there would be no automobiles. And if there were no automobiles . . .

Other passions may cool and other commitments weaken but the romance between Americans and their automobiles appears to have greater staying power than most other attachments—despite such intermittent potholes along the way as OPEC's unkindly hand on the gas pump and exhaust fumes that test the stamina of one's lungs. Why else would a letter from Teheran have arrived at Maryland's motor vehicle bureau on June 27,

1980, a time when the great international question of the day was whether or not the fifty-three American Embassy hostages held by Iranian terrorists would get out of their predicament with whole skins? The letter—from the ranking U.S. official among those being held prisoner, L. Bruce Laingen—was devoted to a matter causing him great concern. His perilous situation? Not at all. Would the Maryland authorities please renew his driver's license which was then on the eve of expiring?

It is probable that any experienced divorce lawyer would understand how Laingen, hoping one day to again be able to take to the open road, could place such high priority on preventing any barrier from coming between him and his car. After all, it isn't that unusual for divorce settlements to be contested more vigorously over the question of who gets custody of the family car than over who gets custody of the children. Even so, it doesn't quite prepare one for the New Jersey couple who tried to trade their fourteen-month-old son for a '77 Corvette they coveted. The police, alerted by the dealer, instructed him to play along to determine whether the offer was a tasteless pretense or whether the couple's parental gas tank was really running on empty. When the police arrived at the dealership they found the infant crawling on the showroom floor and the parents out on the lot putting their license plates on the Corvette they had just traded for.

As the bizarre incident illustrates, the automobile has assumed almost the form of cult worship among its more dedicated devotees. Around the globe the burnt offerings from smoking tail pipes beyond counting mark the multitudes of the committed. And nowhere are the chrome-plated, piston-driven congregations thicker than in America. And yet, even here among the most committed, there are pockets of the unsubmissive who resist bending a knee in the direction of Detroit or the other meccas of the motorcar.

One of the early skeptics was President Theodore Roosevelt who observed in 1905 that he had ridden in a car only twice in his life and that was quite enough for him. His first motorized outing was in 1902 in a purple-upholstered Columbia which, on purely aesthetic grounds, could hardly have been expected to stimulate enthusiasm. However, it was the second ride that really turned him against the automobile—his chauffeur was stopped by police for speeding at the unseemly rate of about 10 miles an hour. (The nation's very first speeder to be nabbed by police—for whizzing along at 12 miles an hour—was arrested in 1899 by a bicycle-mounted New York patrolman.) After that brush with the law Roosevelt declared he would never again ride in a car, later having to eat his words when he became the first President to own a car and the first to drive one.

Another President who belittled the automobile was Woodrow Wilson and he did it in exceedingly harsh terms. In 1907, five years before he entered the White House, he warned his fellow citizens that more than anything else in America the motorcar had "spread socialist feelings in this country" because it exemplified "the arrogance of wealth." However, like Theodore Roosevelt before him, he discovered that it can be foolhardy to make sweeping statements about automobiles. In 1919, despite his earlier condemnation, Wilson bought a Model T Ford. At least his choice enabled him to avoid the "arrogance of wealth."

Like Roosevelt and Wilson before they recanted, the U.S. Army took a look at the motorcar and joined the ranks of the naysayers. A 1908 Army study disparaged the automobile, predicting it would be unsuited to use in war, a miscalculation it came to regret a short time later when World War I demonstrated the fallacy of the prophecy. The German Army was halted at the Marne when the Allies commandeered all the Paris taxis to rush troops to the front; a British leader, Lord Curzon, later declared that the Allies had "floated to victory on a wave of oil." However, even while it predicted a dismal future for the automobile in its 1908 study, the Army was buying a few to transport its brass; in 1909 when New York City billed it for two dollars to license a car for one of its generals, the Army refused payment on grounds that U.S. government property was immune from taxation.

In less exalted circles, too, there was disparagement of the automobile and various measures were adopted to limit its use. Many roads were posted with "No Horseless Carriages Permitted" signs backed by sheriff's deputies to enforce the ban. The very first motorcar in Atlanta, a Locomobile, on its very first outing in 1901 so frightened a mule that the animal kicked it out of commission. An adjoining county, clearly in the mule's corner, promptly passed an ordinance requiring a motorist encountering a mule or horse to halt at least 100 yards away, turn off his engine, and wait until the animal "has passed his machine and is at least 50 yards beyond."

Even one so knowledgeable of and so linked to the automobile as William Phelps Enos—author of the first police manual of traffic regulations and originator of the stop sign, the one-way street, safety islands, and taxi stands—had no faith in the motorcar. He considered it to be just a passing fancy from which the nation would in time recover. He never got behind the wheel of one and remained loyal to the horse for the rest of his days (although his final earthly passage was in the rear of a motorized hearse). Even more surprising than Enos' dismissal of the motor vehicle as a fad was an official pronouncement from city hall of the municipality recognized globally as Automobile City: Detroit. In their statement Detroit's city fathers declared that the horse would never be fully replaced by a mechanical device like a motorcar. Which only proves that whether on a municipal or a Presidential level, politicians are as apt as anyone else to have a knock in their engines.

But for every voice raised to discredit the automobile there was a chorus to hail it, for every skeptic there was a score of believers. By 1898 New York department stores were offering for sale motorcars imported from France where commercial production had already been under way for a few years. (Fifty years later Sears Roebuck tried the same marketing ploy, unsuccessfully, when it offered its customers the ill-fated Henry J compact under the Allstate nameplate.) By 1898, too, American motorists had banded together in fifty clubs across the nation and in 1902 the biggest, most enduring of them all—the American Automobile Association—was founded. So it is clear that at the turn of the century appreciable numbers of Americans were becoming committed to the motorcar.

More skeptics joined the ranks of the committed in 1903 when the continent was crossed successfully, west to east, by two intrepid motorists driving a Winton for 63 gruelling days. A few months later the same feat was repeated in a Packard that took 54 days to span the country. An upsurge in enthusiasm and greater appreciation for the potential of the automobile came in 1906 when the worst earthquake in U.S. history destroyed much of San Francisco and rescue crews commandeered all the motor vehicles in the area to transport survivors to safety. Now there was a rapidly widening realization that to regard the motorcar as just a plaything of the idle rich was to be misled by a glib slogan.

During the 1910 gubernatorial race in California one of the candidates, Hiram Johnson, registered a first in politics by putting his campaign on motorized wheels. He drove his way right in to the governor's office by stumping the state in a car, along the way demonstrating to politicians everywhere that they now had a way to make more speeches, kiss more babies, and pass out more cigars faster and farther afield than ever before. By 1921 Presidential regard for the automobile had made a complete about-face from Teddy Roosevelt's snubbing of it; President Harding declared that the motorcar had become "an indispensable instrument in our political, social, and industrial life." This was not mere platform oratory. The fact is—in spite of a few persistent pockets of diehards—America now had a new dream to cling to, the dream of owning a "machine" and taking to the open road. For millions by Harding's day that dream had already become reality, and those millions were being augmented at an accelerating pace.

One could already perceive the enormity of what was taking place—overwhelming in scope and potent beyond imagining in the extent to which it was beginning to remake the face of the nation and to alter the lives and the life-styles of its citizens. America was turning its tail pipe to the past and motoring into the new age of the car culture. While the nation was molding its new culture it was, paradoxically, itself being molded by it.

The automobile would, before it was through, become both the servant and the master of America. It would mirror the country's genius and its folly, its uniformity and its diversity, its steadiness and its capriciousness. The motorcar would become the nation's obsession, its economic bellwether, and its status symbol. It would reshape the geography of America, reconstruct its cities, transform its landscape, reformulate the very air it breathes. It would affect the way we work, play, eat, even the way we make love. It would change the way we farm (displacing the horse by the automobile denied us manure and thus made us dependent on artificial fertilizers) and it would change the way we shop (having become motorized into mobile consumers we created the shopping mall to cater to our newfound flexibility). It would influence our art and architecture and literature, our music and movies, our schools and our family life.

Society and the automobile would become bonded to one another so firmly, so enduringly, that we would discover a marriage arranged by the Detroit matchmakers would become virtually divorce-proof. So powerful would the bond become that it would seem to have the potential for persisting even after life itself had ended. That inference appears justified by the 36-ton granite replica of a 1982 Mercedes, carved painstakingly over a 17-month period by three craftsmen, to mark the final resting place of a late resident of New Jersey. And the inference is reinforced farther north in Canada by another granite grave marker depicting a Pontiac Trans Am. Explaining the deceased's attachment to the Pontiac, the monument maker describes it as "the greatest love of his life."

Whatever else it might do or it might become, whatever entrenched customs and institutions it might turn askew, whatever new trails it might blaze, the automobile culture would never become dull, never colorless, never flabby. It would sparkle with drama and humor, with fascinating unpredictability, and with human vitality and quirkiness.

Thus, we have indeed heeded the Biblical injunction—we have gone near and have joined ourselves to the chariot. The pages that follow trace a selective road map of the route we have followed in our motorized chariots and give a sidelong glance at some of the more memorable charioteers with whom we have shared the road.

2
The Road to Autopia

Why is his chariot so long in coming? why tarry the wheels . . . ?

—Judges 5:28

Admittedly it calls for some freewheeling imagination but, if you can manage it, visualize a sort of scaled-down, divine Detroit with its very own god running the heavenly assembly line. That is the scene Homer would have us believe that Vulcan, the Roman fire god, created in the dim recesses of antiquity. In his *Iliad* the Greek poet asserts, in his splendid dactylic hexameter, that among Vulcan's other celestial pursuits he built three-wheeled vehicles that rolled from place to place under their own power, "self-moved, obedient to the beck of the gods." In other words, according to Homer, the fire god created a heavenly factory where he turned out automobiles. What seems most remarkable about all this is not the claim that Vulcan was the Lee Iacocca of the deities but that even as far back as the Homeric era men could imagine that indispensable adjunct of modern life, the automobile.

As recently as this century another poet, Thomas Russell Ybarra, whose rhyming doggerel is hardly in the same league as Homer's epic verse, also had a go at draping the automobile in a Roman toga. Tongue-in-cheek, Ybarra put it this way:

Oh, the Roman was a rogue,
He erat was, you bettum;
He ran his automobilus
And smoked his cigarettum.

To a current generation conditioned to believe that life begins at a chromed radiator grille and ends at a growling tail pipe it may seem strange that one is unable to say clearly and certainly where and when and by whom the all-important, all-pervasive automobile was invented, but that is precisely the case. To a greater extent than any other of mankind's great inventions, the motorized road vehicle is a prime example of creeping development, of invention through the slow accumulation of bits and pieces over a period of time so long that one cannot even pin down its commencement with any approximation of accuracy.

The simple fact is that over the centuries so many hands stirred the broth that by magnifying a grain of truth one can expand to impressive proportions the list of those who added a pinch of seasoning to the automotive soup. For instance, the Chinese could put forth a claim—although a weak one—to playing a role in developing the automobile because, according to legend, their ancestors created "fire carts," steam-propelled road vehicles, during the Chou Dynasty around 800 B.C. But anyone bent on joining Homer and Ybarra in bowing in the direction of Rome could present a stronger case.

Proponents of Rome could point to two fifteenth-century Italian contemporaries: Francesco di Giorgio Martini and Leonardo da Vinci. Martini, an engineer by training, designed (although there is no account of its ever having been built) a man-propelled carriage mounted on four wheels, each individually powered by a hand-turned capstan arrangement. A system of gearing was provided to transmit the rotation of each capstan to the wheel beneath it. Although Martini may have been strong on his engineering, he was weak on practicality—the four capstan-turners would have been hung over from fatigue after muscling the carriage along for just a short crawl. But what makes Martini's carriage memorable is that he coined a word for it that nobody before him had used: automobile, from *autos*, Greek for "self," and *mobilis*, Latin for "moving." His design concept for the self-mover faded into obscurity but his word concept for it fared far differently and eventually was elevated into universal acceptance.

The superbly talented and resourceful da Vinci had interests that ranged widely, so it is no surprise that the possibility of creating a self-propelled land vehicle claimed his attention. What da Vinci conceived was an armor-plated vehicle intended for warfare. Oddly for one so brilliant as he, his propulsion system was a parallel of Martini's and so it suffered from the same defects. His concept contributed nothing of any real merit, not even—like Martini's effort—a name. But da Vinci had done so much so well for so long that he has to be granted the privilege of having an off day.

Or take the Dutch, certainly no strangers to harnessing the wind to make it perform useful work, who as early as 1600 employed wind power to propel sail-mounted carriages. Although the carriages are supposed to have carried a score of passengers at speeds as high as 20 miles an hour, it seems probable that the accounts of that period fudged on both the passenger load and the speed. In later experiments the sails were abandoned in favor of small windmills built onto the carriages, with the mill vanes geared to the wheels. However, whether equipped with sails or with windmills, they were never anything more than cumbersome curiosities wholely dependent upon the whim of the breezes. On the other hand, they were probably the first land vehicles to be propelled by anything other than animal or human musclepower (if one accepts that the legendary Chinese "fire carts" did not ever actually exist).

While the Dutch were thinking in terms of the wind, others elsewhere were using different avenues of approach. One idea considered by some was to employ a clockwork arrangement for propulsion. In the mid-1700s a Frenchman, Jacques de Vaucanson, built an experimental vehicle powered by an engine built like the innards of a giant clock. All he really succeeded in accomplishing was to produce a whimsical adult toy. What he had neglected to factor into his calculations was that any clockwork capable of moving a vehicle and its passengers would necessarily outweigh the load it was supposed to carry and thus the whole thing would become an unavoidably self-defeating proposition. Furthermore, winding such a massive clock motor would take a greater toll in time and sweat than it would be worth, even if it were to work. To put it nontechnically, any farmhand could have told de Vaucanson that no matter how long and how hard you squeeze, you can't get ten gallons of milk out of a five-gallon cow.

Another idea pursued was for a vehicle propelled by a compressed-air engine. Inventors in England, France, Germany, and elsewhere worked on the design for several years and although none found the elusive answer to the riddle of self-propulsion, they made important strides in the right direction. It was through their collective efforts that significant fragments of the solution began to fall into place, elements of the ultimate whole like valves, pistons, cylinders, and connecting rods, and an emerging perception of how one fragment related to another.

One has to concede that both truth and chauvinism appear to be on the side of Frenchmen who find joy in pointing out that when you are talking automobiles you are talking French, literally as well as figuratively. Although "automobile" is itself a word of Italian coinage, many of the terms commonly associated with it are unquestionably French—garage, chauffeur, limousine, chassis, and cab (from *cabriolet*) among them. Even more to the point, most historians tend to agree that the first vehicle that could with some logic be called an automobile was the ungainly, heavy, three-wheeled, steam-driven contraption developed in 1769 by Captain Nicolas-Joseph Cugnot, a French Army engineer. (However, Cugnot was actually Swiss by birth, a fact the French would just as soon not dwell on.) Admittedly, Cugnot's creation was slow, ponderous, and progressed by spasmodic fits and starts. In test runs it carried four passengers at a sluggish pace midway between a loiter and a saunter—a little over two miles an hour—and it had to halt every twenty minutes to build a fresh head of steam, enabling operation for another twenty minutes. Yet, despite all its shortcomings it was undeniably a self-powered, steerable, wheeled people-transporter that demonstrated the workability of its concept. Thus it was an automobile, fully consistent with the meaning of the *autos* and *mobilis* that Martini had linked semantically.

Unfortunately for Cugnot, his military superiors were men of limited vision and limited budget. They failed to appreciate the potential of his creation and denied him additional funding to develop it further, so he had to return to other duties. However, when the French put their francs on the barrelhead they insist on having something to show for it; consequently, although believing that Cugnot's vehicle was without genuine merit, the military preserved it and it can be viewed today in the Paris museum, Conservatoire des Arts et Métiers.

Others elsewhere had greater confidence in the value of putting steam on wheels. This was especially so in Great Britain where it was an article of faith that if anyone knew how to master steam properly it was they. After all, it was Thomas Savery, an English engineer, who had given the world its first steam engine in 1698. Granted it was crude, woefully inefficient, and frequently blew up, but Thomas Newcomen, an English blacksmith, had come along in 1711 to turn out a less cranky and less dangerous version of it. Then, in 1769, James Watt, a Scottish instrument maker, had patented a truly improved steam engine that became widely employed in British mines, mills, and factories. And even before Britain had its steam engine it had its vision of a vehicle powered by steam. Sir Isaac Newton, whose formulation of the theory of gravity was only one of his brilliant contributions to science, had as early as 1680 conceived of a carriage propelled by a "rearwardly directed jet of steam." (If Sir Isaac's concept has a modern ring to it, it is because rearwardly directed jets provide the thrust enabling rockets to probe space.) So in 1801 when an engineer in Cornwall, Richard Trevithick, built an experimental road steamer, he was treading a furrow that had already been turned by an English plow, at least theoretically. Two years later he constructed an improved model. In a London demonstration it proved itself capable of sustained, reliable performance at speeds up to its maximum of 12 miles an hour.

Meanwhile, others were working on steam propulsion in Germany, Denmark, Sweden, France (despite French Army disdain for the Cugnot machine), and the United States. American road steamers were built by Apollo Kinsley in Connecticut, Nathan Read in Massachusetts, and Oliver Evans in Pennsylvania. The Evans vehicle,

30 feet long and weighing 15 tons, was intended for harbor dredging and had the distinction of being the world's first amphibious conveyance. On its first run in 1804 it clanked along slowly on huge iron wheels, frightening the scrapple out of Philadelphia gawkers, and then entered the Schuylkill River where its propulsive energy was diverted from the land wheels to a stern paddlewheel.

Initially, it was in Britain that steamers made their greatest impact. By the 1830s they were providing an embryonic network affording passenger and freight service to a handful of cities. The public viewed this with mixed emotions, a large segment complaining that the road steamers were noisy—which was quite true—and dangerous—which was occasionally true. As one might expect, bitterest condemnation was voiced by the vested interests—the horse-drawn transporters and the railroads—who viewed the steamers as potential business competitors. Yielding to this pressure, in 1865 Parliament adopted the "Red Flag" Act that effectively reversed the strengthening trend toward steamers. The Act limited steamers to a speed of four miles an hour on the open road and two miles in cities, and required a three-man crew, one walking ahead displaying a red flag to warn of the approach. Thus stymied by the onerous restrictions, several British engineers turned their attention to electricity as a promising alternative to steam.

The first electric-powered road vehicle is believed to have been built in Scotland around 1839 by Robert Anderson, but it and others built in Britain in the next several years were generally unsuccessful. The concept of the electric was attractive because the engine started immediately, unlike a steamer which had to wait for the boiler to build up pressure, and it ran silently, again unlike the steamer. The drawback was that the electric batteries were bulky, heavy, and unreliable, and had to be recharged after only a short run. The situation improved somewhat around 1880 with development of a longer-lasting battery. But excessive weight and bulk of the batteries and the need for frequent rechargings continued to be limiting factors, although electric cabs did appear on the London streets in the late 1800s.

On the Continent, too, steamers and electrics gained only restrained acceptance. In France the electric had a brief, shining hour of public acclaim when Camille Jenatzy, driving a Jeantaud electric, pushed the cigar-shaped vehicle to a record of 60 miles an hour on April 29, 1899. Unfortunately, the punishing, high-speed run burned out the specially fabricated batteries and when the cheers died away so did French interest in electrics.

It was in America that steamers and electrics gained their most sustained measure of success. Eventually twenty different U.S. manufacturers would produce electrics; in their peak year of popularity, 1912, nearly 35,000 of them would be operating on American roads. But they could not shake their built-in limitations of bulky batteries and short range between rechargings. Steamers enjoyed greater public acceptance. Before the steamer became a museum piece, more than 100 American plants were turning out steamers, most notably the

Stanley brothers' factory in Newton, Massachusetts. The Stanley Steamer was affectionately nicknamed "The Flying Teapot," and with good reason; in 1906 a Stanley Steamer clocked a remarkable 127.6 miles an hour on the sands of Ormond Beach, Florida.

Both the steamers and the electrics were living on borrowed time. They were on a collision course with a third type of road vehicle—an automobile powered by a gasoline-fueled, internal-combustion engine—and they would not be able to survive the impact.

It is not as though the internal-combustion automobile burst forth on the scene all of a sudden to crowd electrics and steamers off the road and into retirement. It had been on the way ever since 1860 when Etienne Lenoir applied to the authorities in Paris for a patent on his invention, an internal-combustion engine fueled by coal gas. In his patent application the French inventor listed the potential usages he foresaw for his engine; among them he included the propulsion of a carriage. Two years later he built such a vehicle to put his idea to the test. Although it was crude, it worked, but it ran so poorly and so slowly—about one mile an hour—that he became discouraged and abandoned his effort.

While Lenoir was having his short-lived encounter with a motorcar in Paris, in Vienna Siegfried Marcus was similarly engaged. In 1864 the resourceful Austrian built a one-cylinder engine that incorporated a rudimentary carburetor and a magneto arrangement to create successive small explosions that applied alternating pressures against the piston within the cylinder. Bolting his engine to a cart, Marcus geared the piston to the rear wheels. Then, while a burly assistant lifted the rear of the cart clear of the ground, he started the engine. The wheels began to turn and each successive explosive pop kept them turning. Signaling the assistant to lower the cart, Marcus watched it burp along for some 500 feet before it ran out of fuel. Ten years later he built an improved version of his motorcar and then, in a curious replay of Lenoir in Paris, Marcus washed his hands of the whole thing, terming the undertaking a senseless waste of time. (In 1950 his second model, preserved in an Austrian museum, was refurbished and taken for a test run in Vienna where it reached a top speed of 10 miles an hour on level ground.)

Despite their considerable shortcomings, Lenoir's and Marcus' crude vehicles demonstrated the feasibility of their concept and suggested the form that road transport of the future might one day take—once the defects and inadequacies had been overcome. But it would be grossly overstating the case to credit them, either individually or collectively, with creating the internal-combustion automobile. When all is said and done, they lacked faith in their enterprises and neither of them had the tenacity to pursue to a fully successful conclusion the undertaking he had begun.

If not Lenoir and Marcus, then who? Closest to the mark in the judgment of most historians is another pair of inventors who had faith in the motorcar and who persevered doggedly until they had found the pieces of the puzzle and had fit them all together neatly. Carl Friedrich

Benz and Gottlieb Wilhelm Daimler, working separately in their native Germany, each designed and built at almost the same moment the world's first commercially successful cars that were in all major respects the direct lineal antecedents of the modern automobile.

Benz produced his initial motorcar in Mannheim in 1885. In appearance, as well as in its initial road test, it was not very impressive. A frail, carriagelike three-wheeler with tubular framework, it mounted a Benz-designed, one-horsepower, one-cylinder engine—a refinement of the four-stroke engine designed by another German, Nikolaus August Otto (which was itself a refinement of Lenoir's two-stroke engine). But that three-wheeler of Benz, frail and awkward though it appeared, incorporated the essential elements that would become characteristic of the modern motor vehicle; electrical ignition, differential, mechanical valves, carburetor, a cooling system for the engine, oil and grease cups for lubrication, and a braking system. Benz was issued a patent in 1886 for his "carriage with gas engine" as it was described in the official grant.

In a suburb of Stuttgart, a scant 75 miles from Carl Benz in Mannheim, Daimler was working diligently on designing a better internal-combustion engine. In 1883 he was satisfied that he had succeeded in producing a more efficient, four-stroke, gasoline-fueled engine and it was granted a patent. (The "gas" engines available earlier had been fueled by hydrogen or turpentine vapors or by coal gas, but in the United States Daimler's use of gasoline had been anticipated by a Bostonian, George

Brayton, who patented a gasoline engine in 1872.) Daimler's initial application of his engine was to mount it in a sturdy bicycle; the two-wheeler operated satisfactorily on its test run in 1885—it was the prototype of the modern motorcycle. Then, in 1887, building on the experience he had obtained with the motorcycle, Daimler installed his engine in a four-wheel, two-passenger vehicle. The test results were encouraging. The engine developed only fractionally more horsepower than Benz's but it did so at a much higher speed—900 revolutions per minute as compared with only 300 for the Benz—and it was the first example of a high-speed internal-combustion engine.

Between them, Benz and Daimler had managed to give the world its first good look at the basic form of the modern automobile. They would continue, separately and competitively, to develop improved engines and more refined vehicles to mount them in. Ironically, when Gottlieb Daimler died in 1900, the management of his company removed his nameplate from the car he had created; the new nameplate they affixed was Mercedes, for Mercedes Jellinek, daughter of an influential Daimler distributer living in France. In 1926 when Carl Benz was eighty-two—he was to live another three years—the rival Daimler and Benz companies merged into one firm. Oddly, the two automotive giants who had paralleled each other in so many ways and who had lived and worked less than 75 miles apart had never met one another.

The two German trailblazers had poised the world for

entry into the Automobile Age. However, as the nineteenth century was making way for the twentieth, the world seemed to show little inclination to take the plunge—except for some pockets of enthusiasts with money enough to indulge their fancy, and except for France generally where commercial production of motorcars was starting to assume some tentative measure of significance. Something more was needed before a windshield would become the world's windowpane. That something would be provided by America.

3
Wheels for the World

I am going to democratize the automobile. When I'm through everybody will be able to afford one, and everyone will have one.

—Henry Ford

It would be a mistake to assume that America had been sitting back on its buggy seat waiting for European ingenuity to show it how to hitch its wagon to a motor. Ingenuity had been at work on both sides of the Atlantic, although it had got going earlier in Europe. From the time in 1804 that Oliver Evans and his steam-powered amphibian had set Philadelphia buzzing, a score of Americans—some of them technically trained engineers and inventors, others just plain shade-tree tinkerers—had been actively engaged in developing motorized road vehicles. Numerous steamers and electrics had been produced, many performing reasonably well, given their limitations. The nation had even recorded its very first repossession—a steamer reclaimed from the Boston buyer after he failed to make timely payments to the builder. By the time Benz and Daimler demonstrated the feasibility of the gasoline-fueled, internal-combustion automobile, some in the U.S. were already working on the same concept. So as the nineteenth century was winding down, the nation already had some automotive expertise under its belt and was ready for more, notwithstanding the fact that portions of the general public remained skeptical of the whole enterprise.

There was ample reason for Americans in general to be receptive to the motorcar. To a striking degree, mobility is a national characteristic. From the time of the nomadic Indian tribes through the arrival of the waves of immigrants, this has been a land of movement until a country a continent wide and half a continent deep was peopled, and even then many would not stay put. So to move was American and it was consistent with that tradition to welcome the enhanced mobility promised by the motorcar.

The railroads, smug and dictatorial in the fiefdoms they had carved out, provided additional incentive for the public to look forward to automobility. Virtually a law unto themselves, the high-handed rail monopolies had provoked widespread public resentment. Now, thanks to the advent of the automobile, the public could contemplate the alluring prospect of a detour around the tyranny of the rail barons.

But a road vehicle without adequate roads is like a five-string guitar with only four strings—no matter how skilled the performer the likelihood of being asked for an encore is remote. And U.S. roads of the period inhibited any encore performances. They ranged from marginal to miserable, and even at that they were in woefully short supply. However, by a fortunate coincidence of timing, the automobile was attaining practicality at the same moment that federal and local authorities were at last awakening to the great need to build decent roads. They had been prodded into wakefulness by farmers demanding accessible routes to take crops to market and by bicyclists (the nation having been caught up in a rage for bicycles) clamoring for roads they could pedal without inviting dislodgement of their vertebrae. It would still be decades before anything resembling an adequate road system would be in place—as late as 1900 the national total of hard-surface roads scarcely totalled 40,000 miles, many of them simply gravelled. The country's first mile of concrete was not laid until 1908; at that time Kansas had just 273 miles of macadam or gravel roads, Delaware had only 66, Nebraska had a mere 23, and Oklahoma had none at all. But at least—Oklahoma aside—a start had been made and in a few states several of the roads had been upgraded from insufferable to sufferable.

Thus, by general inclination and by timing, most of the nation needed little prodding to climb behind the steering wheel.

One enduring aspect of America's reach for the steering wheel is that it is surrounded by a body of colorful mythology with no genuine basis in fact. There is no shortage of examples. Detroit was not the forge in which the U.S. auto industry began to take shape—Hartford,

Indianapolis, Cleveland, and a dozen other places have better credentials for making the claim. Henry Ford did not originate the mass-production techniques that enabled the young industry to thrive; the interchangeability of parts—a key element in mass manufacturing—dates from 1798 when Eli Whitney, of cotton gin fame, announced his opening of a plant in New Haven to fabricate muskets "on the new principle" of standardized, interchangeable parts. Nor is it true that the first American internal-combustion car to go into commercial production was the Ford. However, the real fascination of the automobile does not lie in its mythology. It lies in what actually did happen.

Historians generally credit two bicycle-making brothers in Springfield, Massachusetts—J. Frank and Charles E. Duryea—with designing and producing America's first successful, internal-combustion car in 1892-93, although several crude, experimental motorized buggies had already been built in the U.S. before the Duryea. Actually, to refer to the Duryea as an automobile is a technical accuracy but a linguistic inflation; it seemed to be simply a well-worn, high-wheeled carriage with a small, one-cylinder gasoline engine mounted on its back—which is precisely what it was. The Duryeas themselves, not certain whether they should call it a buggy or an automobile, arrived at a compromise by terming it a "buggyaut." Nevertheless, despite what it looked to be, it did what an automobile is supposed to do: it operated successfully under its own power, although success called for a sensitive hand on the tiller. To steer, one turned the tiller from side to side; to control the speed, one raised or lowered the tiller.

Once they had satisfied themselves that they had the hang of it, the Duryeas busied themselves designing and building a second, better model equipped with a two-speed transmission. Pleased with the way it turned out, the brothers decided to enter it in the nation's first, full-fledged automobile race. Sponsored by the Chicago *Times-Herald*, it was to be run on Thanksgiving Day, 1895.

There were 80 cars entered in the race but only six were able to make it to the starting line: the Duryea driven by Frank, three foreign entries, and two American electrics. The route laid out by the *Times-Herald* commenced in Chicago, turned north along the west bank of Lake Michigan as far as Waukegan, then doubled back to the starting point, a round trip of about 80 miles. The night before the race a snowstorm swept in off the lake, piling up drifts and crusting the rutted roads with an icy glazing. In the best of times road conditions would have been a severe test of car and driver, and this was the worst of times. The race officials wisely decided to shorten the course, making Evanston the turnaround point. Even so, first one and then another of the entries was forced to drop out of the race. Frank in the Duryea kept plugging away. His was the first car across the finish line—54 miles and nine hours after the starting gun went off. The only other finisher was a Benz and as soon as it came to a halt, the driver, undone from the exhaustion of having to push his car so often from ice-slickened ruts, keeled over.

The Duryeas took the $2,000 in prize money the win brought them and with it established themselves as the Duryea Motor Wagon Company, manufacturers of automobiles. Viewed from the perspective of today, it seems astonishing that two bicycle mechanics with only $2,000 in the pot and little more than hand tools to work with could blithely set themselves up as commercial carmakers. (The Duryea remained on the market until 1917.) But that was an era when a dollar was still a dollar and a man who knew how to go about it and was capable of handling tools skillfully could build cars if the spirit moved him—no lawyers and accountants and efficiency experts, no feasibility studies and environmental impact analyses, no bank lines of credit, and no labor contracts.

Many others were quick to follow the lead of the Duryeas. In Kokomo, Indiana, Elwood Haynes drew up plans for a one-cylinder, two-seater and took them around to the machine shop of Elmer and Edgar Apperson for fabrication. It turned out well enough to persuade all three of them that their futures were linked to the automobile. Haynes and the Appersons set up two separate companies to produce competing cars. To demonstrate the reliability of his model, Haynes drove one from Kokomo to New York and return, covering about 10,000 miles in the roundabout route he followed—an impressive feat for the times.

A carriage-maker in Flint, Michigan, William Crapo Durant, became intrigued with the newfangled motorcar and so, benefiting from the experience of others, he put one together. Encouraged by the way it turned out, he turned his back on carriage-making and eventually went on to organize the Buick Motor Car Company, then the General Motors Company, and still later the Chevrolet Motor Company.

George M. Pierce had been earning a comfortable living making birdcages, but the market for cages is not limitless and a career devoted to making them is not so gripping as to claim unswerving loyalty, so Pierce switched to making bicycles when the cycle became a national obsession. Then when the day of the automobile dawned, he easily made the switch to making cars. His company would go on to win plaudits for the fine Pierce-Arrows it would turn out for more than thirty years. Even longer lived would be the Nash that emerged from the tinkering of Charles W. Nash, who could have served as the prototype for the vaunted American rags-to-riches story. He had begun as the humblest of the humble, an itinerant laborer. But Nash had an intuitive feel for machinery, so when the auto came along he could see its potential and could coax some of it into actuality.

They came from everywhere and from every occupation, those early automobile pioneers, some to succeed in carving a niche for themselves in the infant industry, most to falter and eventually fail. White branched out from manufacturing sewing machines to making motor vehicles. Maytag tried for a while and then went back to his washing machines. Steinway bought U.S. manufacturing rights from the German Daimler company and then concluded it made better sense to stick to pianos.

And then there was Henry Ford, a Michigan farmer's son who was determined not to follow in his father's footsteps behind a plow. In 1879 when he was sixteen he knocked the mud off his boots and went to nearby Detroit where he found an opening as a machinist's apprentice. When his apprenticeship was completed he became a steam engine repairman. Later, having gained a reputation for his mechanical skills, he was hired by the local electric company as an engineer.

An inveterate tinkerer, in his spare time in 1896 Ford built an internal-combustion engine from plans he came across in a magazine. Then he built a vehicle to mount the engine in. His motorcar worked—in fact, he put about 1,000 miles on it before he sold it to an acquaintance—but the bicycle-wheeled, tiller-steered two-seater, which had neither brakes nor a reverse gear, was so noisy it was condemned by many as a public nuisance. In 1898 he built a second motorcar. This one was so sufficiently improved over his first that he was able to persuade a few people to back him in manufacturing it commercially. The enterprise failed after only one year.

By this time Ford had become so infected by the automobile bug that no antidote, not even failure, could cure him. He managed to talk a second group of investors into financing a fresh attempt to produce cars for the commercial market. This venture turned out as dismally as the first one had.

An obstinate, highly opinionated man, never lacking in self-confidence, Ford refused to acknowledge defeat. But he was realist enough to recognize that—given his two recent failures—if he were to obtain new financial backers he would have to conjure up something noteworthy to entice them into the fold. That something, he concluded, would need to be a burst of favorable newspaper publicity lauding him for originating an innovative, highly effective car. So he set out to produce something bigger, more powerful, and much faster than anything he had turned out in the past. When he had the vehicle that suited him, he hired a flamboyant, well-known bicycle rider to drive it. The bicyclist he hired, Barney Oldfield, had never driven a car, but Ford considered that to be only a minor problem. He sat Oldfield behind the tiller and schooled him in what to do. The bicyclist was an apt student, displaying the same flair on four wheels that he had flaunted on two.

When he judged his driver was ready, Ford entered him in a race. He had chosen the race shrewdly—it had received a great deal of advance publicity and was to be well covered by the press. Oldfield and the car performed smoothly, coming in first, and Henry Ford garnered the laudatory public notice he had been angling for. On the strength of it he obtained the backing he needed to have another try as a commercial manufacturer. The Ford Motor Company was established in Detroit in 1903. Among the backers were the co-owners of a machine shop, Horace and John Dodge, who were named members of the board of directors in return for their purchase of $10,000 of stock in the new company. Later the two brothers would resign their directorships to start their own automobile company and would cash in their stock for a thumping $25 million. But that was later and this was 1903 with the latest Ford venture far from a sure thing.

When he began his third attempt at manufacturing, Ford knew he was setting out into a minefield. Even though the industry was still very much in its infancy, so many were coming to market with cars that competition for customers was razor-sharp. Even at the very first U.S. auto show, in New York's old Madison Square Garden in 1900, there were already 40 exhibitors offering 300 different models, mostly electrics and steamers. (The most popular car in America that year was the Columbia Electric.) But there had already been a sprinkling of gasoline autos and, in a foretaste of what would become a nagging problem for modern America, there were several foreign imports, mostly French and German. In that same year—1900—there were only 8,000 registered cars on U.S. roads (although the total number was greater, since registration was not yet mandatory everywhere in the country), so it was clear that in such a highly competitive climate the weakest, least innovative producers were bound to fail.

With the market so modest in size, and with it fragmented by so many out to get a piece of the pie, none was able to come away with a decent slice to chew on.

None, that is, until Ransom E. Olds showed the others how it could be done. It wasn't the first time that Olds, a one-time machinist, had led the way.

In 1893 Olds had built a steamer that a Bombay merchant bought for use in India—it was the first recorded export of an American automobile. In 1899 Olds had persuaded a mineowner to invest in setting up the Olds Motor Vehicle Company with the objective of producing gasoline-fueled cars. In 1901 he was ready to begin manufacturing the model he had designed, but he was going to do it in a way none before him had done. Up to that time a cottage-industry atmosphere had prevailed. Owners took their cars to the blacksmith or the bicycle shop for repair if they could not cope with it themselves. When they needed gas they went to the hardware shop where it was dispensed casually in an open container. Those who built the cars did so on a small scale in a highly personalized way, fabricating them from the ground up by making every part of it themselves and then fitting the pieces together by hand—a tedious, slow process that necessarily kept output low and price tags high.

Olds had a better idea. He abandoned the accepted way of operating and in its place instituted a system of contracting with several machine shops to make required parts for him to his exacting design specifications—transmissions from this shop, carburetors from that one, steering gear from another, and so on. In this way he avoided spreading his resources thin and freed himself to concentrate on rapid, economical assembly of parts delivered by his contractors.

Output of the car—a one-cylinder, three-horsepower, tiller-steered model with bicycle-type wheels and a distinctively curved dashboard—was 401 in 1901, more gasoline-fueled cars than any other U.S. plant had turned out in a single year. In 1902 output rose to 2,500 and the next year—when the Ford Motor Company opened its doors—production topped 3,000. Ransom E. Olds had introduced quantity production to the industry and he had cut himself a big piece of the pie. It did not hurt his sales any when Gus Edwards composed a song that soon had everyone singing about what they would do "In My Merry Oldsmobile." What they wound up doing, besides whatever they may have had in mind, was to make Olds a very rich man.

Well aware that he had his work cut out for him, in his first year Ford brought out the Model A: small, lightweight, powered by a two-cylinder, eight-horsepower engine and selling for $850. The next year, 1904, Ford added the Model B, a four-cylinder selling for $2,000. At that juncture the company was operating in the black but was not setting the automotive world on fire. In 1906 Ford added the Model K to its product line. That year and that car were to be important milestones.

First—the year. If one had to select the year in which it became abundantly clear, even to the skeptics, that the American automobile industry had developed a momentum that could not be arrested, 1906 would be a good choice. In January, time for New York's seventh annual auto show, not one but a surprising two competing shows opened their doors simultaneously only one block from each other. In Madison Square Garden there were 220 exhibitors, while in the rival, upstart 69th Regiment Armory show there were 205 exhibitors; together, the two displays showcased about 800 different models. Many of the cars bore nameplates that only the longest of memories can recall—like Lozier, Knox, Elmore, Grout, Schact, Moon, Marmon, Pope-Toledo, Orient, Welch, Oakland (which would later be transformed into Pontiac), Royal-Tourist, Hewitt, and Northern. But several of them bore names that still have a familiar ring—like Buick, Cadillac, Packard, Studebaker (manufactured by two brothers who were blacksmiths before they turned to automobiles, and whose company in 1911 would become the first to sell cars on the installment payment plan) and, of course, Oldsmobile and Ford. The 1906 cars had abandoned the carriagelike look of earlier models and had begun to assume a motor-age appearance. One of that year's models, a Coyote manufactured in California, introduced a power plant markedly different from those of the past: a V-8 engine. That was also the year in which the first tart comment about the automobile salesman, uttered by Mark Twain, was recorded. Interviewed by a New York *Times* reporter, Twain observed that "If I could talk as fast as some of these automobile salesmen do, I could dictate a great many more words and consequently make more money." In its oblique sort of way, Mark Twain's remark illustrates that in 1906 the automobile had become an immutable fact of life.

Now—the car. Ford's Model K, introduced at the Madison Square Garden show, was big, heavy, fast, and expensive—and it was a mistake. Its six-cylinder engine developed 40-horsepower and could push the 2,000-pound vehicle to a top speed of 60 miles an hour. It sold for $2,800 or $2,000 more than that year's Cadillac. But even at $2,800 the Ford Company lost money on every Model K it sold. Under the circumstances it is probably just as well that it sold poorly. Yet, paradoxically, the failure of the Model K turned out to be a benefit to the company as well as a detriment. It was, in fact, the making of Ford.

His experience with the Model K convinced Henry Ford that his soundest strategy for capturing a greater share of the market would be to forget about big, high-priced models and instead to concentrate on producing a light, simple, rugged model that could be sold cheaply. He had a descriptive term for what he was seeking—"the universal automobile." (It is interesting to note that years later Adolf Hitler ordered the development of an identical sort of vehicle and used a very similar term to describe it—*Volkswagen*, "the people's car.")

Thus the year—1906—and the car—the Model K—were pivotal in setting in motion what would turn out to be a revolution in the young automobile industry: the year because it was then that the automobile was affirmed as an integral part of the American scene, and the car because the Model K was a failure.

Ford, who always assigned a letter designation to each of his models, called the new car he intended to produce the Model T. He described in detail to his engineers and designers what he wanted the new car to be and to do, and he outlined some of the ways he had conceived to accomplish those ends: Among his innovative ideas was to fabricate critical, hard-usage parts from vanadium, a superior steel alloy developed in Europe. Another innovation was to install the steering and controls on the left, an arrangement he considered more logical than the right-hand drive that until then had been the industry standard. A third wrinkle was to make the cylinder heads removable to simplify repairs and maintenance.

By late 1908 the Model T had been built and rebuilt, tested and retested, and was ready to go into production. It was powered by a four-cylinder, 20-horsepower engine, had two forward speeds, and a reverse controlled by pedals, was equipped with a throttle mounted on the steering column, and got about 30 miles to the gallon. The Model T's price tag was set at $850. What the sales literature failed to point out clearly was that for his $850 the buyer would get no windshield or top for the open car. Nor would he get headlights, speedometer, or a spare tire. If he wanted any of those items—and he would have to be a virtual mental retardate not to want them—they would be available as extra-cost options. Ford had not yet initiated the policy of any-color-you-want-as-long-as-it's-black, so early buyers could choose their cars in red, green, or baby blue.

The Model T was all that Henry Ford had envisioned: rugged, relatively simple to maintain, and reasonable in price even after allowing for the optional but necessary add-ons. And its left-hand drive made it more convenient to operate than the competition with its right-hand drive that was so awkward in a system where traffic flow was to the right. Customers responded enthusiastically to the advantages of the Model T, confronting Ford with an enviable problem: how to keep pace with demand. New, larger plant facilities were quickly constructed. Production in 1909 was about 10,000 Model Ts, in 1910 it increased to 19,000, in 1911 to almost 35,000, and in 1912 to 78,000, but still supply did not catch up with demand. Clearly, a new, better, and faster way to build cars was urgently needed. In 1913 Ford found the better way.

What Henry Ford and his top managers did was to bring together into one coordinated system techniques of manufacturing that had been pioneered by others and to add some refinements of their own. They had already been utilizing the well-established technique of standardization and interchangeability of parts. From Henry Leland's Cadillac plant they borrowed the concept of work-flow but they improved on the idea. Leland's work crews had pushed each skeleton Cadillac through the plant on a skid, adding a part here, installing a component there, until at the end it was a completed car. Taking a leaf from the Chicago packing houses that conveyed animal carcasses through their plants suspended from motor-driven endless chains, Ford melded the Cadillac and the packing house concepts into a single, mechanized conveyor system that carried the vehicles past work stations rationally spaced along an assembly line. At each station everything associated with a single component of the car was prestacked within easy reach and each member of the crew performed a specific, repetitive task to mount that component in the vehicle. Moreover, each station was laid out in such a way that labor was performed man-high to eliminate stooping and thus to enhance efficiency; improved worker-comfort was only incidental. Conveyor speed was carefully calculated to make the assemblers at each station hustle through their tasks to keep pace with it.

The techniques of repetition, standardization and interchangeability, minimization of worker movement, and mechanical conveyors brought unprecedented economy of time and labor. Output leaped dramatically. When the Ford staff finished fine-tuning the assembly line, it had reduced the time needed to build a Model T from 14 hours to just 93 minutes. As productivity shot upward the cost of per-unit production plummeted, so that the Model T was enormously profitable for the company, so much so that it shaved the retail price and still wallowed in profits. In 1924, when half of all the cars in the world were Fords, the Model T sold for a remarkably low $290 and still the profits piled up.

Modified a bit over the years but essentially as it had been when the first one left the plant in 1908, the Model

T continued in production until 1927. By that time it had become truly Henry Ford's "universal car," as much at home in Timbuktu as in Trenton. During its nineteen years of production one of every two cars turned out in America had been a Model T. The final one to roll off the assembly line was the 15,007,003rd Tin Lizzie—an astounding production record that was not to be surpassed until the Volkswagen Beetle managed to pull off that feat more than a generation later.

Henry Ford did not create either the automobile or the automobile industry. When he built his first internal-combustion engine from magazine plans in 1896 and then mounted it in a carriage, others before him had already built better motor vehicles than his crude attempt. By the time his final Model T rolled out of the factory more than 4,000 different makes of automobile had been produced for the commercial market in 35 countries around the world. In the United States alone 1,500 companies had tried to carve niches for themselves as makers of motor vehicles. But all of them, whoever and wherever they were, however lasting or fleeting their roles on the automotive scene, all must yield center stage to Henry Ford, for it was he who captained the revolution in the way that cars are made. Even more than that, it was he who had jacked up the world and had slid four wheels under it. He had said he would democratize the automobile and when he was through just about everyone would have a car. He kept his word.

Life would never again be the same.

4
Freewheeling Through Life

Americans are broad-minded people. They'll accept the fact that a person can be an alcoholic, a dope fiend, a wife beater, and even a newspaperman, but if a man doesn't drive there's something wrong with him.

—Art Buchwald

Once the world found itself mounted on wheels it stepped on the gas and never—well, hardly ever—looked back. And nowhere has the long, eventful ride been zippier, zestier, and zanier than in America, for when Henry Ford changed the automobile from plaything for the fortunate few to attainable pleasure for the masses he set in motion a social revolution as profound as his industrial revolution. Americans crowded into the driver's seat and then headed off in a multitude of directions eagerly, spiritedly, and with unihibited imaginativeness.

That the automobile quickly became the great American jack-of-all-work is undeniable. But it is equally undeniable that simultaneously it precipitated change in the approach to almost everything that was accomplished away from the workplace. One of the first social changes it wrought was to alter the mating habits of the nation. The realization dawned early in the game that a backseat offered infinitely more scope than a front porch for the amorously inclined. So there was a mass movement of the young—youthful in either age or libido—from the exposure of the porch to the concealment of a parked car. Motorized wooing had already become an established fact even before the Model T assembly line brought the itinerant love nest within cuddling range of almost everyone's pocketbook. When Gus Edwards composed the vastly popular "In My Merry Oldsmobile," it was not long-distance travel he envisioned when he penned two of the song's provocative lines:

> "You can go as far as you like with me,
> In our merry Oldsmobile."

When a tidal wave of Model Ts began to surge out of Ford's factory doors it simply meant the merry Oldsmobile now had an enormous amount of company. So true was this that in 1944 when he wrote *Cannery Row*, John Steinbeck included this memorable observation: "Most of the babies of the era were conceived in the Model T Ford, and not a few were born in them."

The curved-dash Olds and the Model T may have become museum pieces but they have left the world a legacy that has never followed them into retirement. A recent survey of 6,000 British girls by the London magazine *Woman* reveals that half of them report regularly making love in cars. In Los Angeles, where the libido is not merely an instinctive reponse to biological stimulation but is also a highly marketable commodity, a new business enterprise called Tail Dating adds a fresh dimension to the automobile's amatory potential. Upon payment of a membership fee in the organization a motorist receives a bumper sticker in distinctive day-glo colors. If he—or she—spots another car on the road with a membership sticker and driven by someone who stirs up interest, noting the license number and phoning it in to Tail Dating lays the groundwork for a meeting.

Many of the early auto-makers had no qualms about exploiting the appeal of the motorcar as a convenient and portable solution to the logistics of a discreet encounter. The Jordan firm anticipated Hugh Hefner by a few decades when it named one of its models the Playboy. Its 1924 marketing campaign was created around an ad entitled "Somewhere West of Laramie" and depicting a handsome cowboy and a beautiful girl joyously anticipating what lay ahead as they drove toward it in their Playboy. A Brewster of the same period used a heart-shaped radiator grille to project a similar theme. Several car-makers turned out models whose seats folded down and joined to become double beds, promoting them as sleepers, which prompted many a knowing leer. The feature of a 1934 advertising campaign for De Soto was a blowup of an attractive girl, her eyes closed, her arms outstretched, and her back arched against the automobile's hood. Fifty years later little has changed. Sexual overtones have not disappeared from marketing campaigns and the sleeper has now evolved into the plush van sporting enough creature comforts to rival a Holiday Inn.

The role of the automobile in influencing the way Americans played the dating and mating game claimed public attention because it was so clearly apparent, but even though Detroit's assembly lines could justifiably boast of their many innovations, the libido and what to do about it is not among them. At any rate, it was only one of a myriad of ways in which the emerging car culture was changing American society.

Take school busing, for instance, which is usually considered to be a consequence of activism in the 1960s to achieve equalization of educational opportunity among the races. While that is true enough it is not the whole story because the genesis of school busing dates to a much earlier time. It was one of the first direct outgrowths of the motorcar's unparalleled mobility and flexibility. This opened up to farm families the possibility of transporting their children to more distant schools with better facilities and staff capable of providing greater educational enrichment, and they availed themselves of it. This established the concept of busing and it created the transport system to carry it into being. So when later advocates of busing on behalf of educationally disadvantaged minorities came along, they found that both the precedent and the means were already in place.

Or consider the case of consumerism in rural areas. By tradition, and often through necessity, farm families had made many of the things they wore or ate or used. But with the advent of the automobile, shopping in town became readily and quickly accessible. Bringing town within convenient striking range had the added attraction of offering a respite from the solitude of the farm. The enticements were difficult to resist, so more and more they stimulated a dependence on commercial sources to satisfy rural needs. The farm family that once baked its own bread and sewed its own clothes, put up its own food, made its own soap and axe handles, began to do those things less frequently. Instead, the family drove to town to visit the baker and grocer, the clothing shop and hardware and five-and-ten. Thus, the automobile brought rural Americans to the city every day of the week instead of just on Saturdays as in the horse-and-buggy era. It also brought rural America into full-fledged membership in "store-bought" consumer society.

Or take the matter of the feminists' movement that had been making slow and erratic progress throughout the country ever since the 1820s. The advent of the automobile gave the movement impetus for more rapid growth. An inkling of what the future would hold was discernible, especially in retrospect, in 1898 when a woman—Genevra Delphine Mudge—drove a Waverly Electric in New York to become the nation's first known female motorist. The following year she became the country's initial woman race driver by competing in a Locomobile in a New York meet. By a stroke of bad luck, during that race she skidded into five hapless spectators, knocking them down but not injuring them seriously, to insure herself a minor footnote in history as the first American woman to have an automobile accident. In that same year Chicago established a precedent in the nation by requiring that motorists obtain licenses to drive; among the very first Chicagoans to be licensed was a woman. And before Henry Ford had begun to churn out his Model Ts the Women's Motoring Club of New York was already a flourishing institution. In 1909, the club president—Alice Huyler Ramsey—and three members left New York in an open-bodied Maxwell-Briscoe and drove cross-country to San Francisco, arriving at the Golden Gate 59 days later.

But all of this was merely a prelude for what would come later. Women did not really begin to play a significant role in the car culture until Henry M. Leland introduced the self-starter in his 1912 Cadillac. By thus eliminating the physically demanding and hazardous chore of hand-cranking the engine he removed a major bar to women's climb into the driver's seat. (Leland was spurred into making the improvement when a close friend of his died of injuries sustained in the kickback of a crank handle.) Now the automobile presented to women across the country the means as well as the motive to shed their "homebody" image and claim the same freedom of movement that men enjoyed. Successful in their quest for equality, it was natural for them to extend their gains to other areas of life and it was this thrust that helped speed the arrival of modern feminism.

The automobile did more than simply give America a new look—it also gave the nation a new way of looking.

Freed from the tyranny of the fixed schedules and fixed routes of the public transportation systems, now motorists could look at time and distance and see in them possibilities that had not been apparent previously. Now they could travel impulsively, wheeling off whenever they wished to wherever they wished for as long or as briefly as they wished. And they did so by the thousands.

Some geneticists, only half in jest, salute the motorcar for improving the American breed by providing such vastly expanded opportunities for cross-fertilization by the masses of motorists who ventured far afield. Whether or not the automobile improved the breed may be debatable but it is unquestionable that it altered the breed's pattern of movement. A public on wheels was leaving the beaten path to wander into areas that had not previously known many outlanders. The motorcar was becoming an instrument for introducing the country to itself, enabling growing numbers of travelers to gain an understanding of regional differences and to discover a coincidence of values despite the fact that they were expressed with strange accents. Like the newly adopted homogenization of milk to blend uniformity throughout the bottle, in the 1920s it was becoming clear that the developing car culture was beginning to homogenize the nation.

Someone once asked the notorious bank robber, Willie Sutton, why he kept on hitting banks with such consistent regularity. There was unassailable logic in his classic reply: "Because that's where the money is." Businessmen, applying the same sort of reasoning, looked at the growing numbers of cars on the roads and decided to go after them because that is where so many potential customers were. So business took off after the cars.

First came the gas stations, a scattering of them in the beginning and then, as more of the nation took to wheels, an outbreak of them like a rash spreading across the face of the country. Every road junction had its station, and if it were an important junction it might have one on each corner. The mounting traffic was a joy for the station operators to behold but, as vehicle speeds picked up, the beholding had to be done on the fly; the operators were finding out that they needed a way to capture the drivers' attention before they zipped past to take their business elsewhere. So they began building their stations in eye-arresting shapes—tall concrete tepees, bulbous igloos, animal forms, and other architectural aberrations. The Shell Oil Company erected its stations in the shape of a giant seashell. Because man does not live by gasoline alone, adjacent to the stations came the facilities to cater to the needs of the travelers halting to service their cars—the diners and tourist cabins and other roadside businesses.

Once the rhythm of the highways had been placid and the vistas had been bucolic. The automobile was changing that. It was bringing hustle, commercialization, and visual pollution. The landscape was starting to become despoiled by abandoned tire carcasses, by food wrappings and soda pop bottles, by flattened remains of animals who discovered too late the futility of contesting an automobile for a piece of the road, by service buildings gone awry, and by signs designed to get their sales pitches across quickly and succinctly. For brevity and for the distressingly frequent accuracy of their message it was hard to beat the proliferating "Eats—Gas" signs.

And then, in the 1920s, a measure of moderation began to appear here and there. Some, but by no means all, of the highway commercialization began to be a little less blatant. Stung by criticism of their garish stations, many of the oil companies introduced more traditional architecture to their expanding chains of gas stations. Many of the road signs became a little more sophisticated. One astute advertising man, visualizing the highway as a longitudinal billboard, innovated the clever Burma Shave jingles with verse delivered in short bursts on signs spaced out to match the speed of traffic. (However, his very first signs—posted in Minnesota in 1926—did not rhyme.) The tourist cabins were upgraded gradually into tourist courts with amenities that were less austere. And the roadside diner, which had so often represented a form of culinary Russian roulette, began to show signs of improving. Then the first of the highway food chains made its appearance; while it would not cause gourmets to swoon with rapture, at least it did give assurance of a standardized menu prepared acceptably and sanitarily.

That was the good news. The bad news was that at the very same time that the commercialized highway was gaining ground in some respects, it was losing ground in others. The lure of all those greenbacks rolling down the road was a powerful magnet that attracted new enterprises of all kinds, many of them shoddy—beer joints, hot dog stands, "wild animal" exhibits, fortune-tellers, souvenir shops with plaster pink flamingos and off-color postcards, auto junkyards with mounds of battered hulks, and other detritus of the age of wheels. Signs became bigger and more numerous, and they learned how to make their statements in blinking lights and bright neon. The automobile had opened up the means of escaping to the unspoiled countryside and now it was causing the unspoiled countryside to become elusive, so that escape to it was difficult. It was like driving toward a distant horizon that seemed perversely determined to keep receding.

If the automobile altered the pattern of how and where people were traveling, and what they were encountering on the way there, it was also altering the pattern of how and where they were living. Emancipated by their cars, they were no longer shackled to the congested city, so they fled to the suburbs, bought their lawn mowers and barbecue grills, breathed in the fresh air, and looked forward to enjoying the good life. This was the start of what would be known as the bedroom community, that suburban beachhead with its two human high tides daily—one an outflow of breadwinners to their jobs in the city, the second an inflow from the city's workplaces.

What the residents of these new bedroom communities did not foresee was that they were fleeing to suburbia in such numbers that in time they would recreate there the very conditions that had prompted them to turn their backs on the city in the first place: the congestion, the pressures, and the frustrations. Nor did they foresee in the beginning that they would have to duplicate in their suburban havens the city facilities they had left behind: the schools and libraries and churches, the water and fire protection and other municipal services, and the shopping (which would lead eventually to creating that commercial anthill of purveyors of everything from jogging shoes to French fries—the shopping mall). Ultimately they would realize that they had not left the city at all—they had merely uncoupled its moorings and floated it and themselves to a new location to drop anchor and carry on very much as before. But that realization would come later. For now they mowed and barbecued and breathed air not yet fouled by massed tail pipes.

5
A Man's Bucket Seat Is His Castle

Everything in life is somewhere else, and you get there in a car.

—E. B. White

If pastoral America was being cut to the pattern of the new automobile age, so too was urban America. In fact, it was in the cities that the effects of the car culture made their initial appearance. An indication of what would be coming along later was faintly discernible as early as 1899 when Akron police speeded up the business of hauling lawbreakers off to jail by discarding the horse-drawn paddy wagon in favor of a brand-new motorized wagon. In that same year Boston gave a clearer indication of the transformation that was getting under way when one of its citizens opened a "stable for renting, sale, storage, and repair of motor vehicles." This was the country's first garage and other cities and towns followed suit, slowly at first and then in a rush as motorcars became more commonplace. Then the curbs here and there along the city streets began to sprout hand-cranked gasoline pumps to fuel the cars, gradually bringing to an end the haphazard practice of buying gas in open containers in hardware stores. In 1913 the nation got its first regular, citified service station when an all-night drive-in station opened in Pittsburgh. Business was slow on opening day—only 30 gallons were pumped—but things picked up rapidly after that.

Commencing with the pioneering entrepreneur who established an automobile showroom in New York City in 1900, only a half-dozen years passed before all city centers had their new car showrooms, popular drawing cards for throngs of gawkers who aahed over their gloss and daydreamed about themselves as kings of the road. The used car lots followed in the wake of the showrooms, offering less gloss and less kingly dreams but requiring a smaller outlay in return. The country had hardly taken a fair-sized nibble out of the new century before the motorcar had become a prominent part of its cityscapes and an increasingly powerful force in the economics of its urban areas.

Automobiles were doing more than emerging as a major industry in their own right—they were also stamping their own imprint on old-line, established industries. Learning from the assembly lines of the carmakers, manufacturers of a wide variety of other products adopted and adapted Detroit's techniques to their own operations, in the process enhancing their productivity. Even more than that, the auto industry changed the way that consumer goods were bought and sold. It had been the accepted business practice for companies to market their wares to the public on a cash-on-the-barrelhead basis, only occasionally permitting a few of the big-ticket items like pianos to be purchased on an installment payment plan. But in 1911, when Studebaker announced it would henceforth offer its automobiles on the deferred payment plan, it brought greater legitimacy and acceptance to the system as a marketing device, especially after other car-makers—some of them initially reluctant to do so—gradually followed suit. By 1916, in fact, the advertising slogan under which Maxwell was promoting its cars had become "Pay As You Ride." And less than ten years after Studebaker had led the way, some 50 percent of all cars sold in America were merchandised on time payments. Recognizing what a powerful business stimulant the car-makers had unleashed for themselves, other businesses embraced the concept to market their own products. Thus, Detroit not only put cars in ever-increasing numbers on the road, it also put American consumers in ever-increasing numbers "on the books" by making "buy now, pay later" as commonplace as apple pie and baseball.

It did not take very long for municipal authorities around the country to discover that the proliferation of cars was presenting them with a growing problem: how to regulate the increasing density and the accelerating pace of the traffic. Before the automobile had come along only New York City found it necessary to maintain a squad of traffic policemen; it had organized the squad in 1860 for the sole purpose of escorting pedestrians across Broadway. But after cars took to the streets in significant numbers police departments everywhere found it necessary to organize special squads to regulate the flow of traffic. In 1914 Cleveland broke new ground by installing the nation's first traffic light; it had a buzzer as well as red and green glass disks. As traffic woes continued to mount, a new technical profession was created to deal with them: traffic engineering.

Keeping the vehicles moving in some semblance of good order was only a part of the problem; parking them was the other part. When the increase in road vehicles began to outstrip the capacity of curbside space in city centers to accommodate them all, parking garages were built to take care of the overflow on a short-term basis. Then the unadorned parking lot was developed by shrewd businessmen who recognized that they could swell the cash flow from marginally productive properties by merely paving them over. It wasn't until 1935 that municipal authorities, taking a belated lesson from the parking lot operators, realized that a car at rest could be made to pay for the privilege of taking its ease on city streets. It dawned first on the officials of Oklahoma City, who reacted by installing the nation's first public parking meters.

It had long since become accepted by everyone, though perhaps not everyone may have been happy about it, that the automobile was now an established feature of twentieth-century America. However, it took the Great Depression following the 1929 stock market crash to bring real understanding that for most of the nation the automobile had become something much more than simply a convenient way to get from here to there at a faster clip than by horse and buggy—it had become a fixation, a passion, a basic part of everyday life. No matter the belt-tightening brought about by the Depression, those who owned cars obstinately refused to part with them. If it came down to a question of buying a can of beans or a gallon of gas it was often a toss-up as to which would win out. Ailing cars were nursed as solicitously as ailing children, repairs were improvised from whatever was at hand, replacement parts were scavenged from junkyards to be recycled, anything to keep the family car from giving up the ghost. Astute observer of the human condition that he was, humorist Will Rogers declared that Americans would be the first people on earth to go to the poorhouse in an automobile. Rogers did not live quite long enough to discover that he had actually erred on the side of underestimating the strength of the glue that bonded Americans to their cars. The nation was well on the way to becoming the world's first and most thoroughgoing society on wheels. The United States was being transformed into a drive-in nation.

Recognition that the automobile was altering the American life-style was implicit in the flashing sign a California innkeeper erected outside his establishment in 1924. His sign displayed a brand-new word of his coinage, one that would sweep across the country and, ultimately, across the world: motel. Truncating motor and hotel into a single word acknowledged the fact that guests now arrived in cars and that they wanted accommodations designed especially to suit that circumstance—located on or near major highways away from congested city centers and with parking space convenient to each room. What they wanted was to get in fast, to get out fast, and to have an irreducible minimum of distance between the three legs of the traveling public's new triad: themselves, their cars, and the roadway. The motel gave them that.

Simultaneously with the birth of the motel on the West Coast, on the opposite side of the country Florida was innovating another departure in catering to the motorist: curb service dining with carhops to bridge the gap between restaurant kitchen and automobile steering wheel, so that the driver could have his cake and eat it too, in a manner of speaking. (There are some who claim that a barbecue restaurant in Dallas was the first in the country to offer curb service but most of the votes seem to be cast for Florida.) Then, not to be outdone by California's introduction of motel into every driver's lexicon, Florida coined a word of its own for the automobile-oriented dining room: the drive-in. Drive-ins suited life on wheels and they became immensely popular. That they succeeded in attaining the status of a hallowed national institution was demonstrated beyond question in 1941 when the inaugural was held for the annual Miss Carhop Contest to crown the nation's Glamburger Queen.

Even the federal bureaucracy, never especially noted for alacrity in responding to social change, realized that the American and his car were fast becoming inseparable and reacted with a little innovation of its own. What it did was to design and install drive-up mailboxes equipped with chutes angled out to receive letters from passing motorists. The first drive-up box was installed in Houston in 1927.

Life behind the dashboard took a quantum leap forward on Wilson Boulevard in Camden, New Jersey, at sundown on June 6, 1933. As dusk fell *Wife Beware* starring the debonair Adolphe Menjou began to animate a 40-foot-by-50-foot screen erected in a field big enough to contain 500 cars. Hollywood had encountered Detroit and out of that liaison the drive-in movie had been born. In a single night every automobile had become a potential orchestra seat and entrepreneurs were quick to capitalize on it. Before long the night sky from the Atlantic to the Pacific was animated with movie make-believe. At their peak of popularity more than 4,000 drive-in movies flourished across the U.S.

More and more, almost every facet of life was unfolding between two chrome-plated bumpers. Virtually all of the routine activities of the workaday world were being reorganized so that they might conform to a citizenry that had become wedded to its wheels. To make the transformation more sweeping, a refinement of the drive-in concept was developed: the drive-thru. This enabled a motorist to transact his business by driving up to a window in the establishment or by actually driving right through it.

The drive-thru was the brainchild of Ray Kroc, the man who parlayed a 1.6-ounce patty of ground beef into an awesome empire. When he opened the world's very first McDonald's in Des Plaines, Illinois, in 1955, Kroc launched the fast-food era by eliminating the car-hop (and thereby, as a consequence, also eliminating future Glamburger Queens). The innovation, permitting drivers to roll right up to the kitchen window to have their food passed directly to them, was attuned to the quickened pace of the car culture, although nutritionists did not necessarily sing songs of praise for the drive-thru's fast foods nor educators for the drive-thru's fast spelling. It was not until 1966 that a trailblazing McDonald's—in Huntsville, Alabama—actually allowed dismounted customers to enter the premises for their hamburgers.

Nowadays, thanks to drive-ins, drive-ups, and drive-thrus, Americans without ever disengaging themselves from their cherished automobiles are enabled to withdraw money from their bank accounts, to have their prescriptions filled, to buy a bottle of sherry or a banana split, to pay their utility bills, to pick up birdseed, to have their clothes cleaned, their shirts washed, and their film developed. Drive-up facilities for returning library books are old hat, but a recent innovation is a drive-up window where library books can be borrowed.

A burgeoning California supermarket operation resolutely turns away walk-in trade, catering instead to motorized shoppers who receive drive-thru service. In Dallas anyone who is strapped for cash can take whatever is pawnable to a drive-thru pawn shop and wheel away with money in hand.

The automobile culture has even steered its way into the realm of the spiritual. In a number of places—Los

Angeles and Colorado Springs among them—church-goers can pause to pick up their drive-thru breakfasts and then continue down the road to attend drive-in worship services. Sitting in their six-cylinder pews, they can munch quietly and listen reverently to the loudspeakers bringing them amplified, high-test, no-knock religion. The recessional that concludes the service is the deep-throated chorus resonating from the tail pipes of the departing worshippers.

During the 1950s several Massachusetts drive-in movies figured out a way to serve both God and Mammon. They filled their lots on Saturday nights by showing a nonstop succession of films, all for the price of a single admission; then they invited clergymen to hold services early Sunday morning for those who had remained in the lot through the night.

It would appear that nothing is so inflexibly rigid as to defy reshaping it to the mold of the automobile. In at least two places—Atlanta, and New Roads, Louisiana—there are drive-thru funeral parlors. Canted at an angle calculated to enhance visibility, the dear departed is laid out and spotlighted behind a picture window so that the motorized mourners may bid a final farewell in respectful low gear. Thus, portability has been conferred on the last rites, endowing bereavement with a mobility that enables it to become compatible with the demands of the automobile age. Never before has the off-ramp been interpreted so literally.

What emerges as unarguably conclusive from all of this is that from womb to tomb the American way of life has become synchromeshed with the automobile. The nation had begun its surge into the driver's seat when Henry Ford's assembly lines had commenced disgorging his "universal automobile." But today, gazing down on the scene from behind his heavenly windshield, even Henry Ford must be bemused by the overwhelming universality of the car culture he set in motion with his Tin Lizzie.

6
Fallout from the Car Culture

This strange disease of modern life

—Matthew Arnold

Recently a West Coast marketing consulting firm completed an in-depth survey of 5,000 Americans of driving age to determine their attitudes toward the automobile. As one might have predicted with considerable confidence, the investigators discovered that an overwhelming majority of the sampling was enthusiastic about cars and about driving them. Only 13 percent said that they take no pleasure in owning or driving an automobile and would do without one if they could, while the other 87 percent agreed that they enjoy a meaningful relationship with their wheels.

Which other of mankind's mechanical aids has within it the capability of kindling the same warmth of affection in the human breast? Can one ever feel for a refrigerator or a television set what one feels for a car? Of course not. Which helps one to understand how it was that Clyde, of Bonnie and Clyde notoriety, stopped long enough—

even though pursuing G-men were breathing down his neck—to write a letter to Henry Ford. Surely ranking as the world's most unusual, unsolicited love letter devoted to a mechanical contrivance, it was written in necessary haste in 1934 one month before Clyde and his gun-toting, cigar-smoking sweetheart were killed in a police shoot-out. This is what Clyde wrote:

> Tulsa, Oklahoma
> 10th April
>
> Mr. Henry Ford
> Detroit, Mich.
> Dear Sir:
>
> While I still have breath in my lungs I will tell you what a dandy car you make. I have drove Fords exclusively when I could get away with one. For sustained speed and freedom from trouble the Ford has got ever other car skinned and even if my business hasn't been strictly legal it don't hurt enything to tell you what a fine car you got in the V-8.
>
> Yours Truly,
> Clyde Champion Barrow

(In 1947 the automobile for which Clyde expressed such a depth of affection was put on the auction block. Even though it had been wrecked during the shoot-out, the bullet-riddled hulk fetched a hefty $175,000, which suggests rather forcefully that life after death may be an attainable goal for a car.)

The plain fact is that it is no simple task to find an individual who is so adamantly celibate as to be able to withstand the seduction of an automobile. And once those barriers are breached, the damage has been done—having once drunk of the pleasures dangled so alluringly by the car-makers, seldom does he muster either the will or the wish to go on the wagon. Even so, it is difficult to find anyone nearly so smitten with automobiles as was Charlie Harris, a wealthy recluse of Cape Girardeau, Missouri. When he died not long ago, his neighbors were astonished to learn that he had amassed and hidden away from sight, like a medieval sultan safeguarding his harem, an automobile collection of vast proportions. Parked hubcap to hubcap and bumper to bumper in a cavernous building, his accumulation totalled 155 different models, including eight that exist nowhere else in the world and one that had previously belonged to Ronald Reagan before he entered the White House.

Farther west, in Los Angeles, Gino Denti concentrated all of his affections on just a single car but he did it with exuberant abandon. Taking his ordinary, assembly-line 1977 Cadillac, he made it extraordinary. To start with, he doubled its length to 40 feet. Then he equipped it with such additional amenities as a large-screen television set and a complete bar that included an ice-maker and a sink. If he wishes, Denti could entertain 18 guests at a time sitting in well-upholstered comfort in his cherry red Cadillac. A fellow Californian is so enamored of his favorite car, an antique Benz, that he keeps it in his house—not his garage, his house. It reposes splendidly on a deep pile rug he had woven especially for it in colors that complement it.

During the 1930s, when she was the reigning queen of the strippers, Gypsy Rose Lee delighted in driving about in her rare and elegant Belgian Minerva. Her classic 1929 car, one of less than 50 of that model that were produced, boasted a handsome custom-built body, which seems eminently appropriate since its owner's fame rested largely on a beautiful body. The body—the Minerva's—was lined with zebrawood paneling, upholstered in rich leathers, and appointed with solid brass fittings cast especially for it. More recently, the Lincoln division of Ford signed up such masters of high style and costly ornamentation as Cartier, Givenchy, and Pucci to adorn its limousines with luxurious, personalized embellishments.

All of this points up an inescapable conclusion: for whatever reason—whether it is a love affair with automobiles, a yearning for the sybaritic life, a need for a status symbol, or simply a wish to be different—there are people out there who look at an automobile and see something that many of the rest of us miss. Take this business of status, for instance. To those seeking prestige wheels, not only the car itself but everything pertaining to it must reflect status, not least of all where it gets parked. In the corporate world one's relative importance is often judged by the location of his assigned parking space. Executives will maneuver, cajole, and grovel to improve their position in the corporate parking rankings.

Nowhere is the jockeying for parking position more fiercely competitive than in Hollywood where form often takes precedence over substance and where ratings are the key to success or even to mere survival. The first tangible evidence that one had become a person of some consequence around the movie studios is the attainment of an assigned parking slot with one's own name painted on it. By the same token, the unimpeachable evidence that one has fallen from favor and is to be shunned is the abrupt painting out of his name. Presumably joking, although one cannot be certain about that, Mel Brooks once said that the studios keep a squad of painters standing by in the lots to record the names of those admitted to the rolls of the chosen and to obliterate those ousted.

But obtaining an assigned and named space at the studio, critical though it is, is simply the first rung on the ladder of Hollywood clout. Those few who are the truly anointed eventually, if they are lucky and have played their cards right, reach the topmost rung: a slot directly in front of their office. At Warner Brothers the chief executives park in a carefully designed horseshoe arching around the entrance to the administrative building, with the chairman and the president placed side by side in the center of the arch.

Although Hollywood is a place where the most outrageous things can usually be done with impunity, to park in someone else's slot is not one of them. At a minimum the offending car is towed away. At the Ladd studio a vice president uses super-glue to bond a strip of paper over the windshield of any car that is impertinently deposited in his space. And Alan Ladd, Jr., on at least one occasion let the air out of the tires of an offending car.

But Clint Eastwood, living up to his tough-guy movie image, is even more militant in defense of his slot. Incensed to discover another car in it, he once seized a baseball bat and smashed all its windows. It is assumed that it made his day.

It is clear that for a great many owners the automobile has become something considerably more, and considerably more personal, than simply an efficient and useful assemblage of approximately 14,000 bits and pieces. In this auto-centered society it has become something to be defended stoutly, championed unequivocally, and coddled tenderly. We are possessive and solicitious toward our cars. We dote on them. We lavish money on them. We worry about their health and welfare. Let them cough or run a fever and we rush them to be ministered to. We dress them in glove leather and luxurious plush, crown them with sun roofs, adorn them with wire wheels and racing stripes, bathe them and primp them and polish them.

According to the U.S. Census Bureau, during the latest year for which it has compiled figures—1982—we spent $856 million to wash our cars, not to take dings out of their fenders or touch up their chipped paint but simply to run them through the car wash. To put it another way, what we spend annually just to flush the dirt off our automobiles comes to more than twice the value of all the goods and all the services produced in the Republic of Liberia in the course of a year. By anybody's reckoning, that's a lot of suds. But now something new has appeared on the horizon to raise the stakes and give a fresh dimension to cleaning a soiled car: detailing. The detailing shops, begun in California—as one might have surmised—and now beginning to spread over the country, do not merely wash a car; they massage it with lotions and creams, blow-dry it and caress it with chamois, and collect $145 for the 8-hour beauty treatment.

(In an offbeat sort of way, the abundance of American car washes and the newer detailing shops can serve to contrast sharply the ease of life under capitalism versus the rigors of life under communism. Soviet traffic regulations require Moscow's 500,000 motorists to keep their cars washed or pay a 10-ruble fine levied by police who roam the city looking for dirty cars. The law specifies that drivers must clean their automobiles only in the official washing stations that are located in the outskirts of the capital. This poses an impossible problem for car-owners because according to an official Soviet estimate there are so few washing stations that even if they operated nonstop, which they do not, it would take about 100 days for each private car in Moscow to be washed just one time. To compound the misery for Moscovites, police levy a 30-ruble fine against anyone caught washing his car at home and a fine of at least 100 rubles against anyone found washing an automobile in the countryside.)

Something strange usually seems to happen when Californian meets up with automobile. One reacts on the other in ways that don't occur to the rest of the country until some later date. As it is with detailing, so it was with customizing: adorning a car with embellishments that begin where the car-maker's list of available options ends. Customizing started in Hollywood during its gilded years before World War II when the movie stars sought to outglamor one another, sometimes straining good taste and good judgment in the process. In the beginning it was merely a matter of taking a fine automobile like a Duesenberg or a Packard and making it sleeker and more chic by welding the windshield at a more rakish angle and by enclosing the rear wheels within skirts. Then grace began to make way for gross with touches like reupholstering the interior with fur. Leo Carillo, whom fans of a certain age will recall as *The Cisco Kid*, mounted the head of a longhorn steer on the radiator grille of his Chrysler convertible. To be rear-ended by Carillo was to be hoist on the horns of a differential.

In 1939, one inventive customizer, Theodore P. Hall, let his imagination soar—literally. He attached a set of removable wings to a mini-car and geared the engine to turn either the wheels or a propeller. His flying car did manage to achieve rather precarious flight but eventually he abandoned the idea as impractical, which is probably just as well.

After World War II, customizing became democratized—though not necessarily rehabilitated—by energetic teenagers who made their cars over into hot rods, low-riders and high-riders. They chromed everything chromable, painted everything paintable, often with day-glo colors and seldom with restraint, and otherwise expressed their independence and individuality with touches running the gamut from the mildly congruous to the wildly incongruous.

This urge to personalize one's car seems to have become endemic throughout the country but most motorists manage to find ways to satisfy it without taking such drastic action as customizing. Often a pair of oversize dice or a pair of undersize boxing gloves hanging from the rearview mirror, or a fuzzy animal whose electrified eyes shine red when the brakes are applied, will do the trick. In the case of the button-down collar, mineral-water set, it might call for displaying the logos of their schools, clubs, or professional societies. Or the timid driver, seeking all the help he can muster, might make the dashboard a shrine for a Saint Christopher medal or a religious statue. And then, of course, there is the ubiquitous bumper sticker that seems to appeal equally to all drivers.

The first thing to know about the bumper sticker is that it did not start out that way. It wasn't stickable when it first saw the light of day early in World War II. It was attached to the bumper by wiring it on and it carried a single, straightforward message: *Buy War Bonds*. After the war the stickers actually became stickers, gaining glue on their backs and variety on their fronts. Ever since then they have been going downhill or they have been ascending new heights, depending upon one's tolerance for this migratory art form. Virtually every car on American roads seems now to have become a mobile message center exhorting the public to do almost everything of which humanity may be capable, including many things that only those of intellectual or moral frailty would attempt to do. Those who keep tabs on such matters estimate that something like 600 million bumper stickers deliver their assorted messages in the course of a year.

If all else fails to satisfy the urge to personalize one's car there is always that purely American phenomenon known formally as the prestige license plate and referred to informally as the vanity tag. In its own way it can probably be considered the ultimate in individualizing, since it is the motorist himself who creates the sentiment on his tag and he can be quite certain that not another car-owner, at least not another one within the same state, has a license plate exactly like it.

It is entirely consistent with historic precedent that the motorist should create his own license plate; that is exactly how it was in the beginning. The first state to require registration of automobiles—New York in 1901—simply collected a $1 fee and assigned a number to the owner. It was up to him to buy brass numerals, bolt them to a strip of leather, and then attach his homemade tag to his car. Later, the states themselves took over the production of the license plates, using their prison population for the actual work—thus, incidentally, training their inmates in a skill for which there was no employment available on the outside. (Montana once had the words "Prison Made" stamped on its tags until it dawned on state authorities that they projected the wrong sort of public relations image.) In 1937 Connecticut officials, judging that motorists would be quite willing to pay a premium for a new way to place their personal imprint on their automobiles, innovated the extra-cost vanity tag. Not to be outdone, other jurisdictions followed Connecticut's lead.

What the licensing authorities promptly discovered was that along with the added revenue generated by the personalized license plates came a giant problem they had not anticipated: the persistence and the ingenuity of many car-owners in seeking tags that spelled out a provocative or a questionable message. They realized to their dismay that just a few letters, chosen adroitly by an inventive and playful motorist, can readily produce a sentiment embarrassing to the issuing agencies. After having their fingers burned several times the authorities added staff members to study each request carefully to prevent the tasteless from being legitimatized with the state's stamp of approval. The battle of wits between applicants and issuing authorities had been joined—sometimes one side won, sometimes the other.

Most vanity tag requests cause no problems for the states. These are the applications for innocuous and lighthearted letter or number-and-letter combinations usually involving names, nicknames, or puns. Like the New York teacher of French whose license plate reads LE PROF, or the Ohioan whose tag message—URAQT—brings a pleased smile to the lips of all the women he drives past. But many deliver messages better left undelivered. In Texas, for example, a place where citizens are generally accustomed to call a spade a spade in plain English, the request for FECES was routinely granted—and then the tag was hastily recalled when the red-faced authorities realized that not all Texans speak plain English. Georgia officials were similarly embarrassed when they issued, and then snatched back in haste, a vanity tag from an applicant who had asked for 4NICK8. It taught them that all requests have to be verbalized as well as simply read.

New Jersey, priding itself on its vigilance in preventing the unseemly from slipping past its scrutiny, rejected a car-owner's application for HOOKER. The motorist immediately brought action to try to force reversal of the decision. The state reopened the case and considered the pros and cons. In the end the officials had to concede they may have been too zealous as guardians of public morality and they issued the contested tag to the applicant: Reverend Clyde Hooker.

On the other hand, not all car-owners always see things in the same way. While some will do battle to get a specific tag, others will do battle to rid themselves of the identical license plate. In California the motor vehicle bureau is continually beseiged with requests for tags reading GAY or some variation of that theme. But in Iowa when letters on some of the routinely issued letters-and-numbers plates spelled GAY, scores of upset citizens hastily rejected them and paid extra to be issued substitutes.

Even though licensing authorities abroad do not permit motorists to indulge in license plate creativity, they can nevertheless find themselves grappling with the phenomenon. Not long ago a young British model was hauled into court in England for personalizing her license plate. Her tag as issued read 395EXY but she had altered the 5 to an S so that it became 39SEXY. The judge, with the imperturbability and sobriety traditional to the British bench, ignored linguistic aptness of the model's tag in its changed form; instead, he reprimanded her sternly and levied a fine.

In a coincidence of timing, while British justice was dealing with do-it-yourself licensing, across the North Sea in Aarhus, Denmark's second largest city, police were launching a crackdown on an outbreak of a similar nature. What plagued the Aarhus police was the sudden rash of expired American license plates appearing on local Danish cars. In a moment of whimsy, a large downtown supermarket—which persisted in remaining vague about its source of supply—had placed the tags on sale. The old American license plates were an immediate hit and throughout the area they began popping up on automobiles. The car-owners were undeterred by the $40 fine that was automatically assessed against them for displaying the U.S. tag, even though the proper Danish one was also displayed.

Although the foreign officials do not have any give in their attitudes toward the personalized license plate, American authorities are less uniform in their reactions. This ambivalence is particularly apparent when they have to decide where to draw the dividing line between what comes within the meaning of acceptability and what misses. Although New Jersey took a stand against HOOKER, the officials next door in Pennsylvania granted TRAMP without a murmur of dissent. And there can be ambivalence even within the same state—Ohio rejected BOOZE but it issued DRUNKY routinely. This flexibility of attitude was not in evidence among literal-minded Michigan authorities confronting a request from a woman for a vanity tag they had already issued to an earlier applicant. Checking her application to learn what she had indicated as her alternate choice they found that she had written "None" in the appropriate space. The lady was very soon riding around with a license plate reading NONE. However, the saga of Mrs. Selma Ghelberg and her personalized license plates seems clearly to be in a category all by itself.

Proud of her automobile and wishing to place her very own imprint on it, Mrs. Ghelberg decided to obtain a personalized tag for it. In settling on the lettering to be placed on the license plate she followed the lead of her son who had established "No Name" as his CB radio "handle." So she applied at Mount Vernon, New York, for NO NAME tags and her request was routinely granted. That set in motion a chain of events that mystified and upset her.

Mrs. Ghelberg had hardly finished tightening the last bolt on her NO NAME license plates when the mailman deposited at her door several dunning notices for unpaid parking tickets. Mrs. Ghelberg's conscience was clear. She had always been punctilious in obeying all regulations; she had committed no parking infractions and therefore could have no unpaid tickets. She carefully explained all this to the Mount Vernon Police Department which was, of course, skeptical. But Mrs. Ghelberg persisted in her protestations of innocence, so the police finally agreed to look into the matter. The investigation led to an embarrassing discovery.

The inquiry into the matter revealed that every time

an officer wrote a ticket with the name of the offender entered on it illegibly the clerks at headquarters punched it into their computer under a "no name" listing. Mount Vernon is tied into the state's master computer in Albany, so whenever it was informed that a ticket had been issued to "no name" it automatically sent back notification that the NO NAME license plates belonged to Mrs. Ghelberg. Whereupon the police issued yet another parking bill to Mrs. NO NAME Ghelberg. Ultimately, the master computer was taught to have better manners. Perhaps the most ironic twist to the tale is that at the time that Mrs. Ghelberg was computerized onto the wrong side of the law she was an employee of the New York State Department of Motor Vehicles.

Although guilt-by-association-with-computer may be a highly unlikely consequence of obtaining a vanity tag, losing those tags to a thief is not at all unusual. Authorities across the country report that prestige license plates are being stolen in increasing numbers. To make matters worse, motorists with personalized tags are discovering that it doesn't pay to be too brainy. The more creative they are in conceiving a tag that sparkles with originality, the more apt they are to have the tag swiped. On the other hand, of course, the victimized owner may be able to derive some small measure of comfort from this clearly implied salute to his creativity.

7
The Elite Fleet

And in thy majesty ride prosperously. . .
—Psalms 45:4

In 1973 when he became Vice President, Gerald R. Ford declared that "I am a Ford, not a Lincoln." It seems reasonably safe to assume that few would wish to dispute the legitimacy of that statement, whether one chooses to interpret it in its literal or in its figurative sense. However, once he made it to the Presidency he discovered that he had become a Ford *in* a Lincoln because the Lincoln was for a long time the official automobile of the President, a tradition begun by Calvin Coolidge in 1924. (Coolidge's predecessor in the White House, Warren G. Harding, was partial to the Packard.) Until Ronald Reagan displayed a fondness for the Cadillac, the only time since Coolidge's day that the official Lincoln had been abandoned—and even then the estrangement lasted only for the brief trip between the Capitol and the White House—was when President Eisenhower startled everyone by taking his inaugural ride in a gleaming white Cadillac convertible, a switch as surprising to the protocol experts as his exchange of the traditional top hat for the more informal homburg.

The fact is that some automobiles come into the world as merely cars, while some others arrive as Conveyances with a capital C. It is not very difficult to pick out those that are the Conveyances—they have about them an unmistakable aura of prestige or power or prosperity, or some of all three in varying degrees. Those American-made cars that rank the highest in their "P factor" are the Lincoln and the Cadillac. (Oddly enough, both the Lincoln and the Cadillac were conceived and produced by the same man, the brilliantly innovative Henry Martin Leland, who sold his Cadillac company to General Motors in 1908 and then thirteen years later sold his Lincoln company to Ford.) All of the others that contended for a time for their share of American automotive prestige have long since gone out of production. They included contenders like the splendid Deusenberg favored by notables from Howard Hughes and William Randolph Hearst to Greta Garbo and Clark Gable, like the Marmon that won the first Indianapolis 500 in 1911 and then in 1931 was produced in an awesome 16-cylinder model, and like the Cord that was so beautifully and innovatively styled that its design was granted a U.S. patent.

Abroad, too, many of the most prestigious marques have disappeared from the highways. Gone is the elegant Hispano-Suiza designed and built in Spain by a Swiss engineer, hailed by King Alfonso VII as the favorite of all his cars, and adored by the high-spirited, master artist, Pablo Picasso. All Paris was delighted by a Picasso caper of the 1930s: racing around the city in a bright yellow Hispano-Suiza on which he had playfully painted a red hammer and sickle, thus giving the car of the aristocrats a touch of proletarianism. Gone, too, are the superb Bugatti, Delage, Delahaye, and Isotta-Fraschini automobiles. But the car that was the first to bring unabashed luxury, brilliant engineering, flawless craftsmanship and graceful styling to the road—the Rolls-Royce—is still doing what it has for so long done so well.

If logic had come into play, the world's most enduringly prestigious car would be called the Royce-Rolls—it seems clear that it is Frederick Henry Royce who deserves the top billing. He was the engineering genius and the consummate craftsman who produced the car and who then devoted the balance of his life to improving it. Charles Stewart Rolls was the man of intense but transient enthusiasms who promoted the car masterfully until a newer passion held him in its grip. So it was Royce who created the car and it was Rolls who created the legend.

Royce's was the prototypical rags-to-riches story: hawking newspapers in London to help support his widowed mother, studying on his own and attending night school to learn about the newly introduced technology of electricity, inventing an electric doorbell and then peddling it door-to-door, and finally attaining firm financial footing by inventing a dynamo for industrial use. In

1903, when he was forty-one, his attention was claimed by the automobile. Taking the best features from existing models and incorporating them into a single design, he built an experimental car. On its trial runs the carefully engineered, skillfully built, two-cylinder Royce operated reliably and smoothly.

Rolls' was a riches-to-riches story: born into monied aristocracy, educated at Cambridge where he was indifferent to the traditional curriculum but fascinated by technical courses, affluent enough to indulge his penchant for whatever was new and exciting. A nineteen-year-old collegian in 1896, he imported a 3½-horsepower Peugeot from France and began organizing competitive sprints, hill climbs, and reliability runs, driving with enough know-how and verve to win many of them. After graduating from Cambridge in 1898 he cast about for something to do that would be neither an affront to his social station nor a bore. To become a common merchant would have been unseemly on both counts but to purvey the expensive plaything of the upper classes was quite another matter, so Rolls established himself in London as an automobile dealer. His enterprise flourished, allowing him time to continue racing and to take up a newer interest: ballooning.

In 1904, though he was skeptical that a manufacturer of doorbells and dynamos could produce a worthwhile car, Rolls reluctantly allowed an acquaintance to persuade him to visit Royce to look his automobile over. Once he took the wheel of the Royce, experienced its solid yet silky-smooth operation and its surge of power beyond what one would have expected from just two cylinders, he realized it was a gem of design and fabrication. Rolls struck a deal to market the entire output, an arrangement that suited Royce very well because it freed him to concentrate on engineering and production. Nor did he mind that Rolls planned to market the vehicle with a new nameplate: Rolls-Royce.

For the next two years Rolls devoted his energies and his talents to establishing for the Rolls-Royce a credible reputation as an automobile that was unimpeachably sound, both mechanically and socially. Once that had been accomplished he took time to pursue his newest passion: flying. He had already progressed from ballooning to gliding, so the transition to powered flight was relatively easy for him. In early 1918 he became the first man to overfly the English Channel in both directions. Two months later, in a crash landing within sight of the Channel he had so recently conquered, Rolls became his country's first air fatality. His short life, only thirty-two years, had been unusually full and unusually fulfilling for the Honorable Charles Stewart Rolls. In his spectacular death, with all of its attendant publicity, he added another note of singularity to the car that bore his name and that Royce continued to refine and improve.

It was in India that the Rolls-Royce was elevated to the status of *the* car of royalty. When the first model reached Bombay it created a sensation and the princes of the subcontinent began at once to vie with one another in collecting Rolls-Royces with the most luxurious of appointments: upholstered in rare leathers, decorated with gold and silver, and even equipped with jewel-encrusted thrones. The central Indian government ordered eight, and one maharajah maintained a personal fleet of 22. However, the fabulously wealthy Nizam of Hyderabad overwhelmed them all by assembling a collection of Rolls-Royces said to have numbered an amazing 50.

Strangely, no British monarch adopted the realm's most prestigious automobile as the Throne's official vehicle until Queen Elizabeth II accorded it that honor in 1952. Until then every British ruler, commencing with Edward VII in 1901, had placed the royal stamp of approval on the Daimler, designed and built in England under an arrangement with the German Daimler company permitting use of its name. Among those puzzled by the British Throne's seeming reluctance to adopt the Rolls was the legendary Lawrence of Arabia who used nine of them during World War I, each armor-plated and mounting a revolving machine-gun turret, to launch devastating hit-and-run attacks against Turkey's desert forces. When journalist Lowell Thomas asked him after the war what single thing he coveted above all else, the conqueror of the Arabian Desert instantly answered, "A Rolls-Royce with tires and petrol to last the rest of my life."

Though Britain's monarchs were slow to climb into the car, the Russian royal family was not. Virtually every member of the extended Russian royal family owned a Rolls-Royce. (However, Henry Ford boasted in 1913 that two Russian grand dukes owned Model Ts.) Czar Nicholas II, not content with just one, had a matched pair of Rolls-Royce Silver Ghosts. But it was the Silver Ghost owned by the Czar's nephew, Prince Feliks Yussupov, that figured in one of the most curious episodes in Russian history. It happened on December 29, 1916, but it had been building to a climax for ten years, ever since Grigori Yefimovich Novykh—better remembered as Rasputin—arrived in St. Petersburg from his native Siberia.

It was not by chance that he was called Rasputin—the name translates as "debauched"—since he was obsessed by the belief that salvation could be achieved only by sinning, a belief he put into practice energetically. Paradoxically, in spite of his amorality, Rasputin proclaimed himself to be a holy man with mystic powers to heal. Stranger still, there is evidence that by carefully manipulating the power of suggestion and the characteristic Russian superstitious temperament, he did accomplish apparent improvement in the condition of several of the afflicted who sought his help. Czarina Alexandra Feodorovna, desperate to do for her son what court physicians could not—cure him of his hemophilia—sent for Rasputin. The Siberian conducted several highly emotional sessions with the royal heir and convinced Alexandra that he had interposed his healing powers between the boy and his illness. Pathetically grateful, Alexandra turned increasingly to Rasputin for advice on personal and public matters. Exploiting his hold over her, Rasputin managed through her to gain significant influence over Czar Nicholas' decisions on affairs of state.

Prince Yussupov, alarmed by Rasputin's meddling in imperial affairs, conspired with four like-minded officials to do away with him. On December 29, 1916, the conspirators lured him to Moika Palace where they fed him cyanide-laced wine and cakes. When the poison seemed to have no effect, Yussupov pumped several bullets into Rasputin. Then the plotters carried their bleeding but still living victim to Yussupov's Rolls-Royce, after first wrapping him in cloths to avoid bloodying the upholstery—after all, whatever the circumstances, one treats one's Rolls with proper respect. Driving to the bank of the frozen Neva River, they dragged the Siberian out and dropped him through a hole in the ice. Certainly no Siberian peasant before Rasputin, and surely none since, ever went to meet his maker in such grand style: propped on the back seat of a Rolls-Royce chauffeured by a prince of the realm.

(A year and a half later the entire royal family was dead, murdered during the Communist revolution. Oddly, Lenin—the father of communism—owned the very hallmark of capitalism, a Rolls-Royce. Nobody knows what happened to Prince Yussupov's Rolls but Lenin's is preserved in a Moscow museum. There is another Rolls-Royce in Moscow today—the British ambassador's official car; the American ambassador gets around in a Cadillac.)

The years have not dulled the luster of the Rolls-Royce. It continues to enjoy a unique capacity to satisfy the urge for grandeur and prestige among those who can afford the high cost of the genuine article. Now the makers of the Rolls, with an eye on Americans who yearn to possess the grandest of the grand and who have resources to match their cupidity, have just begun producing their new, elongated Silver Spur limousine for the U.S. market. The price tag is a staggering $185,000.

Nor have the years diminished the urge among the exceedingly wealthy—the urge first displayed by India's maharajahs—to own multiple Rolls-Royces, thus distancing themselves from the merely well-to-do who possess only one. Wayne Newton, who struck a bonzana singing in the Las Vegas casinos, owns four of them as well as a gold-plated Stutz once belonging to Elvis Presley who had also discovered that a voice could be a money-machine. Commencing in 1978 when he won the heavyweight boxing crown, Larry Holmes bought an additional Rolls-Royce each time he won a title fight. And in Oregon where Swami Bhagnan Shree Rajneesh maintains the headquarters of a religious sect he leads, he remains true to the tradition of the maharajahs of his homeland by keeping a fleet of 30 Rolls-Royces on hand for his personal use—a fresh one for every day of the month.

Though Rolls-Royce occupies a special niche of its own, it does not have the entire prestige market all to itself. Among the elite makers of exotic automobiles is another British company, Aston Martin, home of the car in which superspy James Bond performs his movie heroics. The Aston Martin Lagonda, selling for a very tidy $150,000 minus James Bondish gadgetry, is virtually handmade—only 240 of them are produced each year by the plant's 315 craftsmen, half of the output destined for the United States. Italy claims a portion of the elite market with three makers of splendid, sporty cars: Lamborghini, Ferrari, and Maserati. The Ferrari and Maserati share a distinction that sets them apart from every other car anywhere: they owe their sleek lines to a noodle expert. Their body styling was created by the same industrial designer, an imaginative conceptualizer who brought joy to Italian food lovers by conceiving a popular noodle design for one of that country's leading pasta makers.

Although elitism on wheels is an expensive proposition anywhere, in Italy it doesn't call for quite as massive an outlay as in Britain. The slick, modish Lamborghini Countach goes for $99,500. Wayne Newton owns one to keep his four Rolls-Royces and his gold-plated Stutz company. Nelson Hunt, the Texas multimillionaire, drives a Maserati Quattroporte that sells for $66,000. The Ferrari 308GTS is, one supposes, a bargain among the exotic since it is a mere $59,500. There is even a way to cut that cost sharply if one is willing to accept certain compromises; F.A.O. Schwarz, the noted toy emporium, offers its customers a scaled-down replica of Daddy's Ferrari—nine feet long and powered by an 11-horse gasoline engine—for only $10,000. In a good week Schwarz might dispose of two or even three of its mini-version of road chic.

Germany's Mercedes, like this country's Cadillac and Lincoln, is not in the same league as the truly prestigious automobiles because it is neither crafted by hand in severely limited numbers nor does it claim as stratopheric a price. This distinction comes across even on the toy level; among the luxury items displayed in the Neiman-Marcus department store is a child-size faithful reproduction of a Mercedes—it goes for a third of Schwarz' Ferrari. But even though Mercedes does not play in the same elite league it is certainly not out of the game. Over the years it has been the automobile of choice of many of the monied and the famed. However, political leaders who opt for the Mercedes don't seem to fare very well. Germany's Kaiser Wilhelm was chauffered about in a handsome Mercedes sporting the imperial eagle on its hood; World War I stripped him of both his empire and his luxurious automobile. One war later Germany's Adolf Hitler rode to his ultimate defeat in a Mercedes limousine. (Hitler was so proud of his country's prestige wheels that in 1939 when Nazi Germany and the Soviet Union signed a nonaggression pact that neither nation honored, he presented a Mercedes—a supercharged sports roadster with a rumble seat—to his fellow stain-on-the-record-of-humanity, Joseph Stalin. After Stalin died, the Soviet dictator's son sold his car to a Swede who later sold it to an Arizonan who at this writing is offering it for sale for an awesome $775,000 although he admits he might be talked into accepting a mere $700,000.) Not long after Hitler killed himself in Berlin, the chancellor of the new German Federal Republic that rose from the ashes of Naziism, Mercedes-borne Konrad Adenauer, saw his country split in two when the eastern half broke away. And Emperor Hirohito of Japan, who owned an impressive red and black Mercedes, came out on the losing side in World War II. So political leadership and the Mercedes appear often to be uneasy companions.

It is especially in Africa that the Mercedes enjoys popularity among the politically powerful, though it seems not to be any more a guarantor of longevity in power there than elsewhere. A new word had been coined in Swahili for the powerful in their Mercedes automobiles: *wabenzi*, which translates as "men of Mercedes-Benz." One of the more prominent *wabenzi* was the Central African Republic's Emperor Jean-Bédel Bokassa who had both his empire and his Mercedes fleet taken from him in a 1979 coup. Six years later *wabenzi* head of state, President Alhaji Shehu Shagari of Nigeria, was stripped of his office and his wheels when his government was taken over by dissidents. But if the "men of Mercedes-Benz" seem to have their problems it is quite a different story for a group of portly, middle-aged women in Togo who are known throughout West Africa as the "Mercedes Ladies."

Twenty years ago the women began making nighttime forays into neighboring Ghana to smuggle vast quantities of that country's fine cloth back into Togo. They ended up by gaining control over Togo's entire textile market. With their huge profits they legitimatized their operations and branched out into many other commercial activities. Millionaires many times over, today they drive about Togo in Mercedes limousines to check up on their real estate holdings, restaurants, supermarkets, boutiques, and other enterprises.

A few years ago as Togolese President Gnassingbe Eyadema was preparing to host a conference of African heads of state, his protocol office was distraught to discover that the government did not possess enough VIP automobiles to receive the visitors suitably. A call for help went out from the presidential palace to the "Mercedes Ladies." Within hours a gleaming procession of Mercedes automobiles drew up at the palace to save the president from embarrassment. It seems safe to assert that never has a group been described as "wheeler-dealers" with more aptness and precision than the "Mercedes Ladies" of Togo.

Automobiles are like wine—on the wheel or in the bottle, some are utilitarian products that falter as they age, while for others the years spread a mantle of enhanced elegance, making them more desirable in maturity than in youth. In an Orlando auction in 1981 a Packard that had sold new in 1936 for about $2,000 went for $350,000. A 1936 Mercedes brought $421,000 at a Los Angeles auction in 1979. And a Kansas auto buff has devoted some 30,000 man-hours to fine-tuning and gold- and silver-plating a 1920 Pierce Arrow that Lloyd's of London insured for $1 million.

Even those with bank balances not robust enough to survive the inroads of acquiring an elitist automobile have managed to find a way to accommodate their fiscal frailty to their automotive appetite—they simply obtain a piece of the car of their dreams. Some collect gearshift knobs or the hood ornaments of prestige marques, some concentrate on the builders' blueprints, the dashboard nameplates, the hubcaps, or other parts of the whole. A suburbanite near San Francisco is into hubcaps. He has amassed a daunting abundance of them; more than 3,000 of the gleaming disks hang in all their shining glory from the walls of his house and the fence surrounding it. On a bright day only the foolhardy approach his front door unprotected by sunglasses. A doctor in New Jersey is noted for two specialties: treating ailments of the cardiopulmonary system and collecting Rolls-Royce and Bentley memorabilia of all kinds.

But this matter of automobile elitism has to be placed into proper perspective because sometimes it gets turned upside down. There is a widespread group of car fanciers who seem to delight in thumbing their noses at the traditional concept of what is required to elevate an automobile to elitist status. Among them a Model T that has been faithfully restored to its original state of ugly will readily command a price several times what Henry Ford was able to get for it in its heyday. And the Ford company's monumental blunder of the late 1950s, the Edsel that faced the world with a radiator grille reminiscent of a chromed toilet seat, has now become something of a collector's item, enjoying a degree of chic that was never associated with it when it was new. (Those who are so inclined may be able to read something into the fact that when he made a Vice Presidential visit to Peru in 1959, Richard M. Nixon used an Edsel as his official vehicle.)

Today an Edsel in pristine condition can command a price four times greater than it brought when it was factory-fresh. One avid collector of Edsels has owned as many as 25 at a time.

Nor is this reversal of snobbery-on-wheels confined only to the United States. The same phenomenon can be found in the very capital of the haughty, London, where such factors as the eminence of one's school, tailor, and automobile determine one's social acceptability. There, on the last Saturday of each month, social snobbery is given its comeuppance by a group of British car buffs who, at precisely eight in the evening, begin their Chelsea Cruise along the Thames River embankment. What is so surprising to first-time observers of the Cruise is that every one of the British drivers is behind the wheel of a social outcast—an American car of 1950s and 1960s vintage. Until about midnight, their tape decks playing the music of Buddy Holly or Bill Haley and the Comets, they wend their way along the course: Plymouths and Fords and Chevys, Mercuries and Chryslers, fin-tailed Caddies and even a Checker cab, all of them well maintained and some of them extravagantly customized. It is enough to cause a twitch in the stiff upper lip of London society's upper crust.

But now a Floridian, Vic Hyde, has succeeded in injecting a whole new dimension into the definition of automobile elitism. Over the years Hyde had managed to assemble a stunning fleet of Rolls-Royces that elevated him to a position of eminence among collectors of prestige cars. Then he abruptly changed directions by selling them all off and using the proceeds to finance the purchase of three-wheeled cars, a maneuver which is akin to swapping Stradivariuses for square dance fiddles.

Three-wheelers had never attracted a great deal of attention in the United States, but in Europe a number of companies turned them out, particularly in the austere days immediately after World War II and especially in Germany where three aircraft manufacturers—Messerschmitt, Dornier, and Heinkel—produced them after the Allies clipped the Luftwaffe's wings. Nobody who has ever seen one of those three-wheelers resembling an egg that has been laid between the wheels of a tricycle will deny that it is the very opposite of chic. Mounting into one is motordom's equivalent of wriggling into a pair of tight jeans—and it is just as unforgiving of a plump rump. At last count Hyde had gathered together about 20 of these pint-size three-wheelers and was having great fun with them.

What it all really boils down to is this: some automobiles leave the plant with an unmistakable air of prestige while some others, given the proper set of circumstances, may acquire in later life a measure of the prestige that they had never enjoyed at birth. It is all a matter of public perceptions. The car-makers are keenly aware of this. They never lose sight of the fact that the perceived image of a car will determine where it is positioned in the automobile rankings, which in turn determines how well and how profitably it will sell. So they are not simply in the business of making automobiles; they are also in the business of making images.

One of their prime concerns in seeking to establish a prestige image for a new car has nothing at all to do with engineering or styling—it is what to call it. They agonize over the choice of an exactly right name just as much as a perfumer who is bringing out a new scent, employing in-house experts and outside consultants to devise one that is distinctive, beguiling, and memorable. Some years ago when Ford was preparing to launch a new line of cars the company hired the eminent poet, Marianne Moore, to create a properly prestigious name for the line. Over a period of months Miss Moore proposed several candidates. One, for an exotic flower found only in Tibet and on a single mountain in Hawaii, was Silver Sword. Another, for the exquisite gold and enamel art objects fashioned in imperial Russia, was Fabergé. A third, for a heavenly constellation in the northern sky, was Aguila. In the end Ford thanked Miss Moore politely, paid her generously, and settled on a name of its own choosing: Edsel. The company had much better luck with its in-house choice for another car: Thunderbird. The company also got away much cheaper—to reward the employee who had proposed the name it bought him a new suit.

Starting out with a list of 400 possible names for a new car it was to bring out, the Chrysler Corporation devoted a whole year to analysis of each by sales staff, designers, advertising experts, lawyers, linguists, and other specialists, slowly whittling away until there was a solitary survivor. Satisfied that the long process had led to the best choice, with appropriate fanfare and high expectations

Chrysler unveiled its Dodge Demon. Almost at once the company was showered with mail from clergymen across the country. "We like your new car," the letters read, "but don't think you'll ever induce us to drive a car called Demon."

Foreign car-makers are just as intent as Detroit on creating the precisely right name for their automobiles. And they are just as likely to stumble as their American counterparts. A prominent Japanese manufacturer discovered that fact a long time ago. In 1911, trying to break into the business, the company obtained financial backing from three wealthy investors: Kenjoro Den, Rokuro Aoyama, and Meitaro Takeuchi. By 1918 the firm was ready to go to market with its very first car. Tactfully solicitous of the three investors who had fathered the company, and at the same time hoping for possible sales outside Japan, management decided on an English-sounding name: Datson, for "son of DAT," the initial letters of the last names of the trio of backers. (However, export was to be a long time in coming; it was not until 1925 that the company sold its first cars abroad—a grand total of just three, and all of them to China.) Gradually it began to dawn on management that it had saddled itself with an unfortunate name for its cars because "son" translates phonetically into Japanese as "to lose money," which was hardly an auspicious image for its products to project. The company bided its time until 1932 when Mr. D., Mr. A., and Mr. T. had all faded from the scene and then it changed the name of its automobiles from Datson to the more felicitous Datsun. But even in its altered form the company was never entirely comfortable with the name, so currently it is replacing it with the company's own name: Nissan. Thus, the Land of the Rising Sun is the place of the setting sun for that country's oldest automobile nameplate.

There is one other Japanese name-change that is well worth noting. It does not have anything at all to do with image-making but it has everything to do with illustrating the Japanese fetish for efficiency that has made that nation an awesome industrial giant. The Toyoda company, named for the family that founded it, markets its automobiles under the Toyota marque. Why the inaccurate Toyota rather than the authentic Toyoda? Because when written in Japanese it requires two fewer brush strokes to write Toyota than Toyoda. That kind of exacting attention to minute detail ought to give Detroit something to think about.

8

Making a Statement in Overdrive

The medium is the message.

—Marshall McLuhan

The automobile that started out during the last century as a mechanical contrivance—innovatively conceived and skillfully executed but nevertheless still only a machine—has evolved in the intervening years into something infinitely more than that. It has emerged in this century with a split personality. While it has developed into society's most used and most ubiquitous personal machine, it has at the same time become so thoroughly interwoven into the fabric of human activity that it has assumed a social role far removed from its function as a sophisticated apparatus. On one level it renders a mechanized service to society; on another level it makes a statement to society. In McLuhan's terms, the automobile medium has become the social message.

For example, consider the way in which the automobile has been utilized as a forum for expressing a social philosophy in the area of labor relations. Charlie Chaplin, who in his later years became increasingly an outspoken social critic and a biting satirist as well as a brilliant comic, used the automobile as a vehicle for voicing a forceful political statement in his classic film *Modern Times*. In that film he condemned big industry for what he deemed to be its exploitation and unfeeling depersonalization of its labor force. To dramatize his contention, he focused his lens on an exaggeratedly relentless speed-up of the workers to synchronize them with the rapid pace of the assembly line, and on a similar exaggeration of the monotonous and robotlike repetition of the tasks assigned to those workers.

In much the same manner as Chaplin, Diego Rivera, the great Mexican artist and social critic, expressed his view of the industrial complex in a series of starkly dramatic murals that are displayed in the Detroit Art Institute. In his murals Rivera depicts automobile workers as machinelike cogs in the assembly-line network that webs its way through Ford's massive River Rouge plant, the world's largest industrial installation. One can't help noting the touch of irony in the matter—society's most widely employed appliance is spawned by the mass-production system and then it is turned, even if only as a symbolic technique, against the system that breathed life into it.

Under certain circumstances the automobile can even be transformed into a religious artifact. In the traditional Chinese funeral an integral part of the ceremony calls for the burning of elaborate paper representations of objects calculated to enhance the afterlife of the deceased. Almost always in a position of prominence among the items committed to the funeral pyre is an automobile, in this way granting to the deceased in the spirit world a highly desired object that has usually eluded him on earth. Particularly admired are the realistically crafted, almost life-size, paper sports cars produced by skilled funerary suppliers.

One can assert with certainty that for a late citizen of the People's Republic of China to receive in the spirit world the gift of a car of his very own will be an absolutely unique experience—unless he happens to be a chicken farmer named Sun Guiying. On May 27, 1984, for the first time in its existence, the government of the People's Republic granted one of its citizens—Sun Guiying—permission to buy a private automobile. Having slowly acquired the necessary funds by selling his surplus chickens on the open market after he had delivered his mandatory quota to the state, Sun Guiying promptly bought a Toyota, to become the first one among his country's more than one billion citizens to possess an automobile of his own.

On a less lofty level than as a religious artifact, the automobile has frequently played a role in literature. In a very real sense the medium became the message as numerous poets and novelists employed the automobile as a means of delivering their commentaries on the human condition. Carl Sandburg wrote his "Portrait of a Motorcar" in 1918 and then nearly twenty years later he returned to the automobile as the centerpiece of his long prose poem *The People, Yes*. And forty years after that poets were still drawing on the automobile as a vehicle for communication—for instance, the provocative 1978 poem by Joyce Carol Oates entitled simply "F—" which stood for Ford.

In 1919 Sinclair Lewis wrote in a lighthearted vein of his adventures in a Model T. Six years later, in F. Scott Fitzgerald's masterpiece, *The Great Gatsby*, Gatsby's cream-colored Rolls-Royce became a primary device through which the author portrayed the cynicism of the post-World War I period. The worn-out, patched, and repatched auto in John Steinbeck's 1939 *Grapes of Wrath* symbolized the plight of the worn and weary migrants. And in 1962 William Faulkner wrote with great humor about human foibles against a backdrop of an automobile, an early Winton Flyer, in his classic *The Reivers*.

As often as not, all was far from sweetness and light when poet and novelist brushed up against the automobile. Some were stimulated by the car culture, but many were provoked and depressed by it. Either way, whether stimulated or provoked, the end was the same: for a long line of writers the car and the culture that flowed from it became prods for them in the creation of a large body of literature.

Even more than writers, the composers of popular music have been attracted to the automobile. They hopped aboard almost as soon as the first one took to the road and they have never dismounted, finding it fertile ground for inspiring songs that are largely sexually oriented. The phenomenon took root with "In My Merry

Oldsmobile" and others of the same era like "On the Back Seat of a Henry Ford" and "Tumble in a Rumble Seat" to "Keep Away from the Fellow Who Owns an Automobile." Ever since then, whenever composers of popular music have dealt with the car culture in their songs, they have persisted in thinking of it in terms of a two-part harmony: sex and the automobile. The implication is clear in a long list of songs from Chuck Berry's "Maybelline," Wilson Pickett's "Mustang Sally," and the Beach Boys' "Little Deuce Coupe" to Grace Jones' "Pull Up to the Bumper" and Prince's "Little Red Corvette."

So thoroughly has the automobile become a device for communicating with the public that even dramatists have figured out a highly original way to join the road show. In 1984 the Los Angeles Music Center and the Museum of Contemporary Art jointly commissioned a number of playwrights to create original ten-minute scripts to be performed in automobiles while they are under way—ten minutes being the time required to drive between the two institutions, barring a traffic jam or a fender-bender along the way. Each performance calls for a cast of two on the front seat, one of them driving and acting simultaneously, presumbly without doing violence to either function. The audience is necessarily limited to three, the capacity of the rear seat of the theater-on-wheels. This new art form raises the possibility that in the future actors may need to know how to apply grease as well as greasepaint.

However, it is in the field of the visual arts that the automobile has attained its most sweeping influence as a form of cultural expression. Almost at the very moment that the Museum of Contemporary Art in Los Angeles was infusing new meaning into the expression "a moving performance," it was also mounting an extensive exhibit entitled "Automobile and Culture." The exhibit included 30 cars and 150 works of art depicting aspects of the car culture. After the show closed in Los Angeles it was sent on tour in the United States and in France. There was singular aptness in sending the exhibit to France because it was there that the remarkable painter who was so short of stature and so long of talent, Henri de Toulouse-Lautrec, started the whole thing. He appears to have been the very first to recognize the artistic possibilities inherent in the automobile and to capture on canvas his view of the implications of what would become the most expensive consumer product ever mass-produced. In his 1896 lithograph, *The Motorist*, one can almost hear the deep-throated roar of the car's exhaust as the driver, crouching forward, causes it to spurt ahead.

Following Toulouse-Lautrec's lead, others both in the United States and abroad, took up their brushes to portray the essence of the automobile as they saw it. Some used their brushes in almost cartoon fashion to depict it as a plaything for the idle rich, thus boiling the wastrels in artist's oils for their social irresponsibility. Some, like Toulouse-Lautrec, saw the motorcar as a representation of mankind's dynamism and vitality. Some saw it as a symbol of technological enhancement, while others viewed it as technological debasement. Andy Warhol, who could look at a Campbell soup can and see art where most of the rest of us see only lunch, painted a series of canvases devoted exclusively to gruesome car crashes. Other artists with different social and philosophical axes to grind used the automobile and its culture as motifs for canvases illustrating their varied points of view. And some, leaving social commentary aside, simply saw in the automobile a graceful form and flowing line that constituted man-made beauty and they depicted it as such with no attempt at preachment.

Several artists have dispensed entirely with the process of reproducing the automobile on canvas. They simply let the car speak for itself so that it is its own art form and the medium and the message become truly one. The sleekly styled, futuristic Avanti, designed by Raymond Loewy in 1962 in a fruitless effort to keep the Studebaker firm from bankruptcy, has been displayed as a work of art by the Smithsonian Institution in Washington and by the Museum of Modern Art in New York, which has also displayed several other cars solely on the basis of their artistic merit.

In 1964 a Dodge was the focal point of a controversial art exhibit in Los Angeles that ignited a fire-storm of outraged public protest. The Dodge itself was noncontroversial enough. The cause of the furor was the two manikins the artist had sculpted and had placed on the backseat in a sexually explicit pose. All efforts to have the automobile banned from public showing on the grounds of obscenity failed. However, museum officials agreed to a compromise solution in which the rear doors of the Dodge were closed.

The most visited, most photographed, and most talked about example of auto-as-art is unquestionably an outdoor exhibit just off Interstate 40 about a cupful of gasoline east of Amarillo, Texas. Motorists who are unaware of what lies ahead are puzzled as their approach brings them their first glimpse of reflected sunlight glinting from ten objects lined up at the edge of a wheat field. When they draw close and realize what they are seeing they invariably step on the brakes and get out for a closer look—which seldom manages to banish their puzzlement. Before they continue on their way they will, if they are like most, take photos and quite possibly scratch or lipstick a little graffiti on what is an exhibit that has attracted wide international attention.

What they are viewing is a collaborative effort of three waggish artists: the Cadillac Ranch as it is called and as it has been immortalized in a Bruce Springsteen song of the same title. The trio of creators unveiled the Ranch on June 21, 1974, but instead of raising longhorns it raises long tails: a line of ten Cadillacs buried nose-down as deep as their windshields in the Panhandle loam, their tail fins reaching sassily for the sky. The cars range in vintage from 1949 when tail fins were just starting to sprout, to 1964 when tail fins—having grown without restraint or good taste—were finally shrinking. The stars of the lineup are clearly the '55 and '57 models, the most extravagantly finned of the lot. Weather-beaten and rusted, paint flaking away where it hasn't been scratched off, upholstery tattered, the Cadillacs constitute a clear exposition of the artists' intent to burlesque the excesses of Detroit. Beyond that, they leave the impression of a line of overendowed, overused, and overage chorines straining for one last high kick while they still have the strength for the effort.

Out on the West Coast there is a notable echo of the Cadillac Ranch idea. Perched on a setback above a trendy Los Angeles restaurant is a Calypso green, 1959 Cadillac with its fins flaring in salute to those passing through the entrance below. The automotive theme is paralleled with unusual appropriateness by one of the restaurant's backers—Willie Nelson whose musical trademark is his hit song "On the Road Again."

The three playful artists who conceived the Cadillac Ranch look with disfavor on the restaurant's foray into automobile art, considering it to be an unfair takeoff of their concept. In an attempt to get the green Cadillac shunted onto an off-ramp, they brought suit against the restaurant in Los Angeles Superior Court. After languishing on the court docket for a year the suit was dismissed in 1984.

More than others elsewhere, Californians seem to be unusually receptive to the idea of the automobile as an artistic statement. Up the coast from the Cadillac-crowned restaurant another car of the same make has been taken in hand by a sculptor who could perceive possibilities in it that were never apparent to its General Motors builders. The sculptor, calling on a crane operator for logistical support, turned his Cadillac over on its side and then raised it aloft impaled on a shining, 20-foot stainless-steel spike. It is an arresting sight that often causes speeders to ease up on the accelerator pedal.

In San Francisco, not far from the neatly shish-kabobbed Cadillac, a restaurant has one-upped the downstate establishment that has its car sitting above the entrance. This one has its automobile right inside the dining room. It is the restaurant's sole decoration. But it isn't just sitting there quietly looking arty—it is crashing into the wall. And it isn't just an ordinary car—it is a police cruiser. The message, if there is one, is elusive.

What all of this ferment of auto-as-art really represents is not readily explainable, but that it should bubble up more readily and spiritedly in California than elsewhere is not particularly surprising. Californians seem to grant their cars a remarkable degree of latitude. After all, that is where a prime-time television series called "Knight Rider" is produced and anyone who has ever seen a segment knows that the sleekly handsome star of the show is an automobile that outtalks, outthinks, and almost always outacts the merely human members of the cast. And one should not forget that in California even motherhood is within the realm of possibility for an automobile, if the basic assumption of the TV series "My Mother the Car" is to be believed. At least this 3-speed, 6-cylinder parent had the good sense to project a sultry voice—supplied off-camera by actress Ann Sothern.

9
Reflections in Neutral

Our national flower is the concrete cloverleaf.
—Lewis Mumford

By the mid-1970s it had become increasingly apparent that for some of us the thrill was gone, or—if not yet gone—it was fading fast. At long last the great American love affair with the automobile was simmering down into what was coming more and more to resemble a marriage of convenience, a marriage too unsettling to arouse great enthusiasm yet too practical to be disavowed. It was as Samuel Johnson, speaking in another context, had said two centuries earlier: "Marriage has many pains, but celibacy has no pleasures."

Why the change? What had gone wrong? Some—the hard-core autophiles who remain fully committed to their wheels—would say nothing had changed, nothing had gone wrong. They continue to be enamored of the automobile, heedless of the social observers who theorize that anyone who loves a machine has a flaw in his love-life. However, for most of us the rose-colored glasses have come off and the automobile has come to be seen more clearly for what it is really meant to be:

wheels to get us from A to B. That doesn't mean that we don't want to get to B in comfort and in style. But it does mean that we now understand, despite the beguiling words of skillful advertising agencies that would have us believe otherwise, that the car is a mechanical appliance, not a magic carpet, and that it exacts from us a price not printed on the window sticker. It is a price we pay in manipulation by the manufacturers, the petroleum producers, and the special interest lobbies; in a natural environment that has become degraded; in product unreliability that tries our patience, saps our pocketbooks, and consumes our time; and in other ways that niggle and annoy us. To fully appreciate that price and to understand how it got that way one must start by looking at some of the statistics of the car culture.

Automobile numbers are awesome in size and they are surprising in scope. Some of the figures are depressing in their implication, and a few are downright frightening in their significance. Considered all together, they expose the extent to which our society has become intertwined with and dominated by the automobile. Here are some of the measures of that dominion:

There are about 130 million passenger cars on the streets and highways of the country. They vie with each other and with 40 million vehicles of other types for a piece of the nearly 4 million miles of American roadway. By comparison, the Soviet Union—with a population 40 million *greater* than the United States—has 113 million *fewer* cars. Admittedly, cars are not easily available or affordable in the Soviet Union. So consider the situation in ten Western countries—Belgium, Denmark, France, Great Britain, Holland, Italy, Norway, Sweden, Switzerland, and West Germany—whose combined population matches the Soviet Union's and where automobiles are as available and affordable as in the U.S. and where, moreover, they took to the roads earlier than in America. In spite of all this, there are 29 million fewer cars in those countries combined than in the United States alone. In fact, Americans own about 40 percent of *all* motor vehicles in existence anywhere in the world. Four out of every ten American families own two or more vehicles. (It usually comes as a surprise to learn that the country with the second largest number of cars is Japan, even though only fifty years ago it had less automobiles than were registered at that time in St. Louis alone.)

If appreciating the massiveness of the number of cars in the United States is difficult to grasp, it may come into sharper focus by concentrating on just a single part of those vehicles: their wheels. As those wheels roll along the highway, friction with the road surface causes minute specks of rubber to flake off the tires. In the course of a single year those tiny fragments add up to over 400 million pounds of rubber.

Almost as many automobiles are stolen annually in the United States as there are registered in all Norway—about one million. In Boston alone roughly as many cars are lost to thieves in a single year as there are registered in Nicaragua. (According to the FBI, the model most frequently targeted by thieves is the Buick Riviera, followed by the Celica Supra, the Cadillac Eldorado, and the Chevrolet Corvette.)

Once every seven minutes someone somewhere in New York, tired of nursing a car wracked by a case of terminal disrepair, simply abandons it on the city's streets. In the most recent year for which data are available more than 77,000 New Yorkers walked away from their cars, leaving the remains for the sanitation department to inter.

According to the 1980 U.S. Census of Population, 83.5 million Americans in that year traveled to work each day in an automobile. Getting to the workplace, or to any other place, by car is only a part of the equation; the other part is parking the vehicle once the destination has been reached—and this has emerged as a nagging problem for authorities wherever the car culture flourishes. Paris police report that one-third of all cars parked on that city's streets at any one time are left there illegally. In Japan before a car can be registered the owner must prove to police that he has bought or rented a parking space for it; a space in central Tokyo rents for about $130 a month—a sum that would be considered a bargain by a New Yorker who must pay more than $400 a month to rent a space in central Manhattan. Washington, Philadelphia, and some other American cities are so frustrated and wearied by their mountains of outstanding parking tickets that they have been forced to employ outside collection agencies to try to whittle them down. Chicago is choking on its unpaid parking tickets—more than 500 million dollars' worth—and each year it writes another 4 million tickets. The enormous sums—either those uncollected or those spent in policing, administering, and adjudicating, and the flourishing of a scofflaw attitude and of opportunities for bribery and corruption—make it clear that even with its engine turned off an automobile creates monumental problems for society.

Where does one find the most automobiles per capita? Likeliest would seem to be Los Angeles where exhaust fumes regularly vanquish the rays of the sun; instead it turns out to be quiet, little Casper, Wyoming, which has 729 vehicles for each 1,000 inhabitants against only 596 for each 1,000 Angelenos. On an area basis, however, Los Angeles has the greatest density of automobiles of any place on earth: 3,040 cars per square mile. On the other side of the continent, more cars enter midtown Manhattan each day than there are registered in Wyoming, Vermont, and Alaska combined.

It is this automotive density in America's metropolitan regions that so alarms many who view the motor vehicle as a voracious competitor for our living space, compressing us into an ever-diminishing area. In his 1971 classic, *The City in History*, Lewis Mumford—the respected urbanologist—writes that "Los Angeles has now become an undifferentiated mass of houses, walled off into sectors by many-laned expressways, with ramps, and viaducts that create special bottlenecks of their own. These expressways move but a small fraction of the traffic per hour once carried by public transportation, at a much lower rate of speed, in an environment befouled by smog, itself produced by the lethal exhausts of the technologically backward motorcars. More than a third of the Los Angeles area is consumed by the grotesque transportation facilities; two-thirds of central Los Angeles are occupied by streets, freeways, parking facilities, garages. This is space-eating with a vengeance." (Mumford could have added that the space-eating that goes on outside the house continues within its walls; the average American house with garage attached devotes 15 percent of its space to the owner's car or cars.)

Mumford's words are exceedingly strong stuff but they find widespread agreement among many urban authorities. Since he wrote his words, the situation has not shown any improvement. Automobile density has worsened. More open spaces have been sacrificed to make way for the infrastructure needed to accommodate the increased vehicles. While it is true that Congress adopted the Clean Air Act in an attempt to eliminate harmful emissions, it is also true that the catalytic converters mandated by that Act suppress certain emissions but at the same time substitute others that are causing worry. A recent issue of *New Scientist,* a responsible and highly regarded British journal, raises concerns that the converters may well be health hazards, pointing to Swiss research indicating that their emissions may cause cancer.

Although the degree of lethality of the rear end of an automobile may be open to debate, there are no such doubts raised about the havoc wrought by its front end. According to the National Highway Traffic Safety Administration there were approximately 155 million licensed drivers on U.S. roads in 1984. In fourteen of the states a license can be obtained by those as young as fourteen if the parent or guardian grants permission. That means that roughly two out of every three Americans has the legal right to operate a motor vehicle on the public highways. Sadly, it is apparent that for a significant segment of those drivers their motor vehicle becomes a lethal weapon. This has been the case almost from the first moment that an American motorist climbed into the driver's seat. In 1896 a New Yorker out for a spin in his Duryea collided with a bicyclist and broke her leg; the victim went to the hospital and the motorist went to jail. It was an intimation of things to come. Three years later another New York driver struck and killed a pedestrian alighting from a streetcar—the nation had now sustained the first in what would mount to a tragic toll of fatalities.

The National Transportation Safety Board reports that 44,175 people were killed in automobile accidents on American roads in 1984. In addition, a staggering 1,600,000 accident victims sustained disabling injuries, 150,000 of them of a permanent nature. Comparing these figures with the casualties incurred by U.S. forces in Vietnam brings the matter into sharp, melancholy focus. During the nine years of the Vietnam War the total American battle dead was only about 2,000 greater than the number slaughtered on American highways in the single year of 1983, while the number of battle-wounded requiring hospitalization was less than one-tenth the number of those disabled by automobile accidents in the U.S. during the same time periods. In fact, more Americans by far have been killed by cars since that first fatality in New York in 1899 than have been killed by enemy action in all the wars this nation had ever fought. That, more than any other single statistic, surely must make plain that America's love affair with the automobile is star-crossed, that there is a dark side to this romance.

Another measure of the extent to which the car culture has grown into such an overwhelmingly dominant factor in modern American society is to assess the economic impact it exerts on all of us. One way to approach the economics of life on wheels is to consider how big a bite it takes out of each motorist's pocketbook. A study released by the Hertz Corporation in 1985 reports that despite falling gasoline prices and increased fuel efficiency the typical costs of driving an American car continued to mount—to an average outlay of 45.67 cents per mile for a compact and 59.77 cents for a standard-size car. Based on driving 10,000 miles a year—a typical figure—and including costs of depreciation, insurance, licensing, usual repairs, accessories, gas and oil, the total comes to over $4,500 annually for a compact and almost $6,000 for a standard. Any financing charges incurred along the way would increase those totals to even more. So the bite just for direct operating costs of a car is not merely a dainty morsel, it is a greedy mouthful.

Another way to appraise the economics of the car culture is to evaluate it in relation to the country's gross national product, the total value of all of the goods and services produced throughout the nation. Here the enormity of the automobile's dollars-and-cents role is made starkly apparent. A remarkable one-fifth of America's gross national product, either directly or indirectly, is derived from the automobile industry. Thus, it is an overwhelming economic factor.

Depending upon which set of economists you listen to, one worker in every five, every six, or every seven in the U.S. labor force is employed in an automobile-related activity. There are all of the obvious activities like manufacturing, repairing or servicing the vehicles; marketing, insuring or financing them; renting them out, parking them, or ticketing them; or catering to the creature needs of those who travel in them. But there are also car culture activities that generally escape recognition. For instance, marble workers have a stake in the health of the automobile market because some 100 pounds of pulverized marble—as much as 200 pounds in the case of certain models—go into the fabrication of a car to strengthen the synthetics used in trim, seat backs, and fender liners. What this means to the marble industry can be gleaned from the fact that one major American quarry alone ships some 1,300,000,000 pounds of pulverized marble to Detroit each year.

The contemporary car is a complicated amalgam of about 14,000 parts. The majority of those parts are fashioned of expectable materials like steel, glass, rubber, and aluminum. But a surprisingly large number call for materials that, like marble, seem to be remote from the needs of a motor vehicle. Among them are gold, silver, ceramics, and silicone for electronic components; mica for high-gloss paints; tungsten and mercury for lighting systems; palladium and rhodium for catalytic converters; jute for backing floor coverings; and cork for gaskets. Thus, no matter how one chooses to approach the question of the economic implications of a motorized America the conclusion is clear: if Detroit gets a headache the whole nation has to reach for the aspirin bottle.

In essence then it comes down to this: the nations' love affair with the automobile has undergone a gradual change over the years, becoming something quite different from what it was in the beginning. It has matured into a complex relationship that raises troubling questions. For some of us, of course, the old fire and passion may still be there, unweakened by reservations and doubts. But others of us have lost our wide-eyed innocence, replacing it with varying degrees of disillusionment and unease. But for all of us—the innocent and the disillusioned, the impassioned and the passionless—there is no turning back. In today's world the automobile has become an inevitability—like a sneeze, even if you feel it coming on and wish to stop it you can't.

Some years ago Dr. Philip Handler, the articulate and quick-witted president of the National Academy of Sciences, was buttonholed at a Washington reception by a young woman who expressed deeply felt condemnation of the scientific community, charging that it forced society into a technological straitjacket where human values count for little. She was especially critical of the automobile as a technological menace to social well-being, enumerating all of the ways in which she perceived it to diminish the quality of life. She concluded by asserting that, all things considered, society would probably be much better off if it had never abandoned the horse in favor of the automobile.

"If I may be permitted just one technological observation," Handler replied, "the horse is unfortunately not a closed-circuit system. How would our expanded society be able to function, or even to survive, solidly entombed beneath a mountain of horse manure?"

Not so very long ago one of the popular bumper stickers carried this rear-end philosophy:

AMERICA—LOVE IT
OR LEAVE IT.

However, the philosophy of the sticker cannot be applied to the vehicle that displays it. You can't love your automobile or leave it, not in a society whose life-force seems to be generated somewhere between the chromed radiator grille and the growling tail pipe. Thus, the conclusion is self-evident: love your automobile if you can but if you can't, at least make the best of the union because it is surely here to stay. No question about it—what Detroit hath joined together no man can put asunder.

Index